W9-AHT-238

ESSENTIAL CHEMISTRY

CHEMICAL REACTIONS

ESSENTIAL CHEMISTRY

Atoms, Molecules, and Compounds

Chemical Reactions

Metals

The Periodic Table

States of Matter

ESSENTIAL CHEMISTRY

CHEMICAL REACTIONS

KRISTI LEW

CHEMICAL REACTIONS

Chelsea House
An imprint of Infobase Publishing
132 West 31st Street
New York NY 10001

Library of Congress Cataloging-in-Publication Data
Lew, Kristi.
Chemical reactions / Kristi Lew.
p. cm. — (Essential chemistry)
Includes bibliographical references and index.
ISBN-13: 978-0-7910-9531-7 (hardcover)
ISBN-10: 0-7910-9531-2 (hardcover)
1. Chemical reactions—Juvenile literature. 2. Chemical reaction, Conditions and laws of—Juvenile literature. I. Title. II. Series.

QD501.L655 2007
541'.39—dc22 2007027736

Chelsea House books are available at special discounts when purchased in bulk quantities for businesses, associations, institutions, or sales promotions. Please call our Special Sales Department in New York at (212) 967–8800 or (800) 322–8755.

You can find Chelsea House on the World Wide Web at http://www.chelseahouse.com

Text design by Erik Lindstrom

Cover design by Ben Peterson

Printed in the United States of America

Bang NMSG 10 9 8 7 6 5 4 3 2 1

This book is printed on acid-free paper.

CONTENTS

Fireworks, Fireflies, and Fuel Cells

Besides starting with the same letter, what do fireworks, fireflies, and fuel cells all have in common? If you said that they all involve **chemical reactions**, you are correct.

Chemical reactions happen all around us, all the time. If you have ever seen a rusting car, a frying egg, or tree leaves turning vivid colors in the fall, you have observed a chemical reaction. If you have ever eaten a slice of toast, then you've eaten the product of a chemical reaction.

There are many different kinds of chemical reactions: Burning wood, dyeing cloth, baking bread, an engine running, and human digestion are just a few examples. There are many, many more. This book will explore these and other examples of chemical reactions and explain how **atoms**, the basic building blocks of everything in the universe, interact with one another to make chemical reactions happen.

Figure 1.1 Examples of chemical reactions. a) This truck's iron frame has rusted over time due to outdoor exposure. b) The chemical composition of this egg changes when it is dropped into a hot pan. c) Fall leaves change color because of the chemical reactions that occur within their veins.

FIREWORKS

With all of their noise, different colors, and different patterns, fireworks light up the summer sky and put on a fascinating and exciting display. But how do fireworks work?

Firecrackers have been around for at least a thousand years. The first firecrackers, believed to have been developed by the ancient Chinese, were made up of black powder (also called *gunpowder*), stuffed into bamboo tubes and tossed into a fire where they made a loud pop. Today, gunpowder is stuffed into a cardboard tube and a fuse is used to light the black powder. Italian *firemasters* are credited with inventing the shells that allow aerial fireworks to be launched into the air and explode in a shower of color.

The deafening explosions and beautiful colors are made possible by combining many different **elements** and **compounds**. Remember that atoms are the basic building blocks of all things. There are more than 100 elements. Each element is made up of only one type of atom. All elements are listed on the periodic table of the elements. Compounds, on the other hand, are substances that are made up of two or more elements.

A good example is black powder. Seventy-five percent of black powder, the substance responsible for lifting a firework shell into the air, is made up of the chemical compound potassium nitrate (KNO_3). The combination of letters and numbers, KNO_3, is potassium nitrate's **chemical formula**. Chemical formulas are a shorthand method that chemists use to describe chemical compounds. The K in KNO_3 stands for the element potassium, the N stands for nitrogen, and the O is for oxygen. When the three elements are written together in a chemical formula, it means they are joined together by chemical bonds into a compound.

In addition to potassium nitrate, black powder contains 15% charcoal, which is made up mostly of the element carbon. The remaining 10% of black powder consists of the element sulfur. The charcoal and the sulfur serve as fuel for the explosive reaction.

Figure 1.2 Fireworks owe their brilliant colors and booming sounds to chemical reactions. Various elemental combinations give fireworks their distinctive qualities.

The potassium nitrate is an **oxidizing agent**. Oxidizing agents are chemicals that can supply oxygen atoms needed for **combustion**, or burning.

The colors that light up the sky during a fireworks display are due to unique combinations of elements and compounds. When fireworks contain aluminum or magnesium, for example, they will burn brighter. When the aluminum is heated, it produces bright white and silver sparks, like the ones seen in sparklers. The elements lithium and strontium give fireworks a characteristic red color. Compounds containing sodium produce yellow or gold fireworks. Copper produces blue and barium produces green. Calcium-containing compounds burn orange. Titanium and iron are used to make sparks, and zinc produces smoke clouds. The element antimony is used to create a glittery effect. Who knew there was so much chemistry involved in making baseball games, state fairs, amusement parks, the Fourth of July, and New Year's Eve celebrations so much fun?

FIREFLIES

Fireworks are not the only chemical reaction lighting up summer night skies. Fireflies trying to attract a mate will put on their own version of a light show every night. These little flying beetles flash lights on their abdomens in order to communicate. Each firefly species has its own unique flashing pattern. There are about 175 different species of fireflies in the United States, and scientists have identified about 2,000 different species, worldwide.

Along with helping the firefly find its mate, the chemical light show also helps to protect it from predators. Fireflies are filled with a nasty tasting chemical called *lucibufagens*. Once a predator gets a mouthful of it, they remember it. Predators learn to associate the fireflies' glow with the nasty taste and will not try to eat them again.

But how in the world do fireflies get their bellies to glow? Cells in the firefly's tail make an **enzyme** called *luciferase*. Enzymes are proteins inside the body that can make chemical reactions happen faster. Inside the firefly's body, the luciferase finds another chemical called *luciferin*. When these two chemicals react with oxygen in the fly's abdomen, they cause a chemical reaction that gives off light.

Organisms that can produce their own light, such as fireflies, some types of bacteria, and certain deep-water fish, are called ***bioluminescent***. While most bioluminescent animals are always emitting light, the firefly is unique because it can actually control when its light goes on and off, how often, and how fast. In male fireflies, the ability to control their lights with precision seems to be especially important: Scientists have discovered that female fireflies in some species prefer males who flash the longest, while females in other species go for males who flashed the fastest. Either way, it seems, female fireflies prefer "flashy" males.

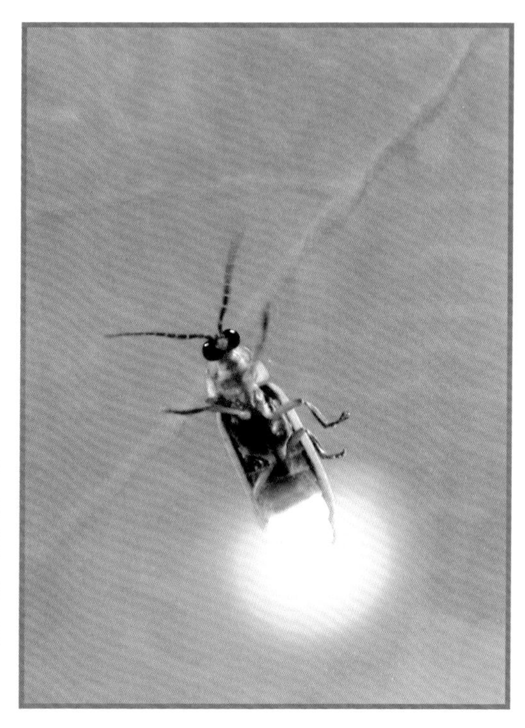

Figure 1.3 A firefly's unique glow is the result of a chemical reaction. Each species has its own "flashing pattern."

Scientists have also found the gene in the firefly's DNA that makes it produce the enzyme luciferase. Medical researchers can now use this information to implant the firefly's light-producing gene into the cells of other animals, including humans. This process could allow the researchers to trace the cells containing luciferase throughout a patient's body. For example, researchers could implant the light-producing gene into cancer cells. Then, if the glowing cells disappear during treatment, researchers would know that their efforts to rid the body of the cancer cells are working.

FUEL CELLS

Chemical reactions can sometimes be used to make **electricity**, too. A fuel cell, for example, uses the chemical reaction between hydrogen and oxygen to produce electricity. Devices that make electricity by using chemical reactions, such as fuel cells and batteries, are called ***electrochemical devices***.

To understand how electricity is formed, it is important to first understand what an atom is made of. All atoms are made of **subatomic particles**. Subatomic particles are particles that are smaller than atoms. The basic subatomic particles that make up atoms are **protons**, **neutrons**, and **electrons**.

Protons and neutrons are found in the dense center, or **nucleus**, of atoms. Protons have a positive electrical charge and a mass of 1 atomic mass unit (amu). The number of protons in an element's nucleus distinguishes that element from any other element. In other words, different elements have a different numbers of protons, and all atoms of the same element have the same number of protons. The **atomic number** of an element shows the number of protons in the nucleus of an atom of that element. So, for example, the atomic number of hydrogen (H) is 1. That means that every atom with a single proton in its nucleus is an atom of hydrogen. Oxygen's (O) atomic number, on the other hand, is 8. This means that all oxygen atoms have 8 protons in their nucleus. The periodic table shows all the elements, arranged in horizontal rows in order of increasing atomic number.

Neutrons are found in the atom's nucleus, too. Neutrons are subatomic particles that have no charge, but they have a mass that is almost equal to that of a proton. Since the nucleus contains protons, which have a positive charge, and neutrons, which are neutral, the nucleus of an atom has an overall positive charge. Most of the mass of an atom is concentrated in its nucleus. In fact, the **mass number** of an element is the sum of the protons and the neutrons in the nucleus of that atom. So, for example, the element chlorine (Cl) has an atomic number of 17, and most chlorine atoms have a mass number of 35. Since chlorine's atomic number is 17, this must mean that all chlorine atoms have 17 protons. Because the mass number is equal to the number of protons plus neutrons, chlorine atoms that have a mass number of 35 must have 18 neutrons—because $17 + 18 = 35$.

All atoms contain one other type of subatomic particle: electrons. Electrons have a negative charge and almost no mass. They are found outside of the nucleus of the atom. In a neutral atom, the negative charge of the electrons must be balanced by the positive charge of the protons. In a neutral atom, then, the number of electrons equals the number of protons.

Electrons are necessary for electricity to form because electricity is the result of electrons in motion. Inside a fuel cell, electrons are stripped of hydrogen atoms that enter the cell. These electrons are now free to travel through a circuit and provide electricity. Remember that hydrogen's atomic number is 1, so it has 1 proton. A neutral hydrogen atom, then, must also contain 1 electron so that the charges balance. In a fuel cell, the stripped-off electrons and the other part of the hydrogen atom—the proton—are eventually combined with oxygen. This combination makes water. Because water is the only byproduct of this reaction, fuel cells produce very little pollution, unlike other methods used to produce electricity.

As long as there is a constant flow of hydrogen and oxygen into a fuel cell, it will provide electricity. Batteries are another, more familiar electrochemical device. Unlike a fuel cell, however, all the chemicals needed to make electricity are carried inside the battery. Eventually all the chemicals are used up, and the battery "goes dead."

Due to an increased concern about global warming, public, government, and business interest in alternative energy sources, including fuel cells, has increased. But more research is needed before fuel cells will be reliable, efficient, and inexpensive enough to replace other ways of generating electricity.

The chemical reactions taking place in fireworks, fireflies, and fuel cells are just the tip of the iceberg. But what exactly is a chemical reaction, and how does one happen?

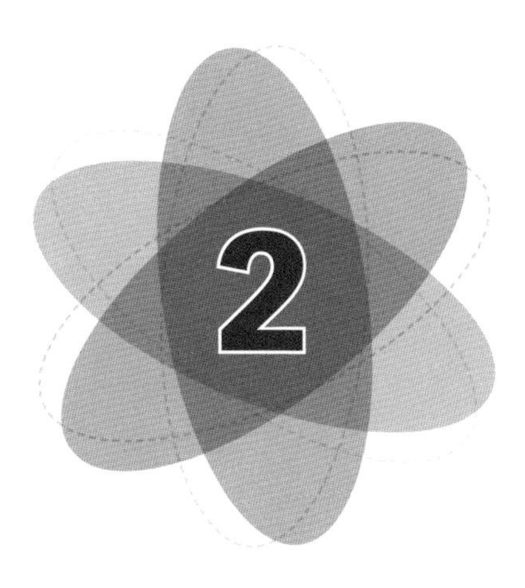

What Are Chemical Reactions?

If two or more elements or chemical compounds come into contact with one another and there is enough energy present, a **chemical change** may take place. When a substance undergoes a chemical change, the chemical structure of that substance is altered. A chemical change can also be called a *chemical reaction*. During a chemical reaction, a new substance is formed.

Burning a log in a fireplace is an example of a chemical reaction. When the wood burns, it reacts with the oxygen in the air. This chemical reaction forms ash, water vapor, and carbon dioxide gas. The wood and the oxygen in this chemical reaction are called **reactants** because they react together to form new substances. The new substances—ash, water vapor, and carbon dioxide—are called **products** because they are produced by the reaction.

Figure 2.1 When two or more substances are combined, their chemical reaction creates new substances. When fire ignites wood, for example, the resulting products are ash, carbon dioxide gas, and water vapor.

Some chemical reactions, such as the explosion of fireworks, happen very, very fast—in less than a second. Others, like the rusting of a car, might take years.

PHYSICAL CHANGE OR CHEMICAL CHANGE

There are also many ways substances can be changed without a chemical reaction taking place and changing the chemical composition of the substance. These changes are called ***physical changes***.

Cutting up a piece of paper is an example of a physical change. The paper is different: It is now in small pieces instead of the larger piece it started out as. But the chemical composition of the smaller pieces of paper is the same as the chemical composition of the larger piece of paper: This is a physical change, not a chemical one. Physical changes are usually easier to reverse than chemical ones. The large piece of paper can be restored, for example, by taping or pasting the small pieces of paper together again. Bending, breaking, and crushing are other ways to change **matter** physically.

Millions of things in the world are matter, because matter is anything that has **mass** and takes up space. All matter is made up of atoms and it usually exists as a solid, a liquid, or a gas. That means that matter has volume, which, in turn, means it takes up space. The mass of an object is defined as a measure of the amount of matter that the object contains. For example, a bowling ball and a ping-pong ball are both made up of matter. But a bowling ball contains more matter than a ping-pong ball, so the bowling ball has more mass. Mass is usually measured in kilograms.

Another thing that is measured in kilograms is the weight of something. Well then, what is the difference between weight and mass? Not a lot, as long as an object remains on Earth. But, if it is taken into space, the object's weight and its mass might be very different. That is because the weight of an object not only depends on the amount of matter it contains but also on how strongly gravity pulls on it. Mass, on the other hand, depends only on how much matter the object contains. So, if an astronaut were to take a bowling ball out into space, away from any gravitational field, and let it go, the bowling ball would just float away because it would have no weight. But its mass would stay the same because it is still made up of the same amount of matter, whether it is out in space or here on Earth.

Now that the difference between mass and weight is cleared up, back to physical changes: Another example of a physical change is when water is frozen to make ice. Ice has the same chemical composition as water. No new substance has been formed. If the ice is melted, it becomes water again. Changes of state, from a solid to a liquid, or from a liquid to a gas, for example, always involve a physical change rather than a chemical one. Most of the time, changes of state can be easily reversed by either adding or taking away heat.

Many, but certainly not all, physical changes can be reversed. Look for words like *boil, freeze, melt, condense, dissolve, break, split, crack, grind, cut, crush,* and *bend* to indicate that a physical change has taken place.

On the other hand, when a chemical change occurs, the original substance cannot be gotten back as easily as liquid water can be turned back into ice. That is because **chemical bonds** are broken and rearranged when a chemical reaction takes place. Chemical bonds hold atoms in a particular arrangement. When they are broken and rearranged, a new substance is formed. It is possible to reverse a chemical change, but only through more chemical reactions.

So, the key to deciding whether it is a chemical or a physical change that has taken place is to determine whether a new chemical substance has been formed or not. One thing to look for is whether energy is being given off or taken in. In some chemical reactions, energy is given off in the form of light, heat, sound, or electricity. When wood is burned it gives off both light and heat. This is an indication that a chemical reaction is taking place.

Giving off energy is not absolute proof, though, because energy can also be released or absorbed in a physical change. In order to melt ice, for example, some heat must be absorbed. In order for water to freeze, some heat must be released. Remember that ice to water and water to ice are examples of physical changes of state, not chemical changes, because water and ice both have the same chemical composition. So it's clear that giving off energy is not enough evidence of a chemical change. More information is needed to determine whether a change is a chemical one or a physical one.

Other ways to tell if a chemical reaction has taken place include looking for the presence of a new material (gas, solid, or liquid) or color. Sometimes a gas will be formed during a chemical reaction. Bubbles of gas can be seen. If the substances involved in a chemical reaction change color, this might also indicate a chemical change.

THE HOUSE THAT CHEMISTRY BUILT

Many things that are required to build a house rely on chemical reactions. Concrete, for example, is a mixture of cement, sand, and gravel or crushed stone. When water is added to this mixture, a chemical reaction called ***hydration*** takes place. During hydration, the compounds in the cement form chemical connections with the surrounding water molecules. Concrete is a popular building material because it is resistant to wind, water, rodents, and insects. It is also non-combustible, which means it will not catch fire.

Carpet fibers are made by chemists in a lab who use a series of chemical reactions, too. Carpet fibers are chemicals called ***polymers***. During the chemical process of ***polymerization***, individual molecules, called ***monomers***, are linked together to form long chains. The prefix *mono-* means "one" and the prefix *poly-* means "many." Knowing this makes it easier to remember that monomers (individual molecules) are joined together to make polymers (many monomers joined together).

In the chemical reaction to create polymers, chemists use catalysts to decrease the amount of energy it takes to create a bond between individual atoms of each monomer. Catalysts are chemicals that speed up chemical reactions.

Chemists also make the paint that goes on the walls of a house. Paint is a thixotropic substance. *Thixotropic* means that the paint liquefies when it is subjected to shearing forces. In other words, the paint is thin and easy to spread as long as the paintbrush is stroking the paint onto the wall. But when the brush strokes stop, the paint thickens.

Figure 2.2 Chemical reactions are different from physical reactions. Physical reactions simply alter the physical characteristics of a substance. Chemical reactions create entirely new products, such as this yellow substance formed by combining two liquid compounds.

If two clear liquids are mixed together and they form an insoluble solid, called a **precipitate**, a chemical change has probably taken place. The precipitate is a new substance that was not present in either of the two clear liquids. The only way to be absolutely sure a chemical change has occurred, though, is to do chemical tests and see if a new substance is present.

A physical change can be thought of as a change in appearance only. If a person were to cut her hair or change the clothes she was wearing, for example, she would have undergone a physical change. But, she is still the same person. She can reverse the physical change by letting her hair grow back or by changing back into the clothes she had on before. A chemical change, however, would change the person into somebody else entirely.

CHEMICAL EQUATIONS AND CONSERVATION OF MASS

When the elements hydrogen and oxygen react with one another, they make water. To write this chemical reaction in words, it would look like this:

$$\text{hydrogen} + \text{oxygen} \rightarrow \text{water}$$

This is called a ***chemical equation***. In a chemical equation, the reactants are always written first, on the left-hand side of the equation. The products are written on the right-hand side. A chemical equation uses an arrow instead of an equal sign as in a math equation.

Chemical equations can also be written using **chemical symbols**. Chemical symbols are a shorthand way to write the name of an element. The chemical symbol for hydrogen is H, and the chemical symbol for oxygen is O.

The reactant side of this chemical equation, using chemical symbols looks like this:

$$H_2 + O_2$$

CHEMISTRY IN THE KITCHEN

All the fabulous success stories and the terrible disasters that can occur in kitchens around the world can be blamed on chemical reactions. Cakes are light and fluffy because the baking soda in the batter reacts with an acid to produce carbon dioxide, a gas. When sugar is heated, it turns into dark brown, gooey caramel. The cut surfaces of apples and bananas turn brown because they react with oxygen in the air. All of these are examples of chemical reactions in the kitchen.

When food is cooked, it goes through chemical changes that alter what it looks like, what it feels like, and how it tastes. Different cooking methods result in different chemical reactions and, therefore, a different look, taste, and feel.

If food is heated over 300°F (154°C), it turns brown. This is why food that is boiled never browns. When food is boiled, its temperature never gets above 212°F (100°C), the boiling point of water. Food fried in oil gets brown, though, because oil boils at a temperature that is higher than 300°F. This browning is called the *Maillard reaction* and is caused by a chemical reaction that takes place between the amino acids and the sugars present in food when food is heated above this temperature. The Maillard reaction is named after the French chemist Louis Camille Maillard, who discovered it in 1912.

Flavor chemists are chemists who develop new food flavors by combining natural and artificial ingredients. A flavor chemist is just one type of food scientist. Food scientists are always searching for better ways to prepare, present, and preserve food.

The H stands for hydrogen and the O stands for oxygen. The small number "2," written below the line, next to the H, means that two atoms of hydrogen are chemically connected together.

Remember that a chemical formula uses chemical symbols and numbers to show the kinds of atoms of each element that are joined together. The chemical formula for water is H_2O. This means that two atoms of hydrogen are chemically joined to one atom of oxygen to make a **molecule** of water. A molecule is the smallest unit of a chemical compound that still has the same chemical properties of the compound. When there is only one atom in a molecule, such as the oxygen in water, the numeral "1" is not written but is just assumed to be there.

The difference between a compound and a molecule can be confusing sometimes. Molecules, like compounds, are composed of atoms joined together by chemical bonds. Remember that compounds are made up of two or more elements. However, the elements fluorine, chlorine, bromine, iodine, hydrogen, nitrogen, and oxygen are known as **diatomic elements**. Diatomic elements always contain two atoms of the same element joined together by chemical bonds. The chemical formulas for these diatomic elements are: F_2 (fluorine), Cl_2 (chlorine), Br_2 (bromine), I_2 (iodine), H_2 (hydrogen), N_2 (nitrogen), and O_2 (oxygen). A hydrogen atom, for example, is never found by itself in nature. It is always joined with another hydrogen atom. All of these diatomic elements are molecules, because they are made up of atoms that are chemically joined. But they are not compounds, because compounds are made up of two or more different elements, and diatomic elements contain only one type of element. All compounds are molecules, but not all molecules are compounds. A molecule can only be a compound if it contains at least two different elements.

Water is both a molecule and compound, and in its case the two words can be used interchangeably. The entire chemical equation showing the formation of water looks like this:

$$H_2 + O_2 \rightarrow H_2O$$

From this equation, a chemist would be able to tell that two joined atoms of hydrogen react with two joined atoms of oxygen to produce water.

This chemical equation is not quite finished, though. That is because in a chemical reaction, atoms cannot be created or destroyed—just rearranged. And if the number of atoms on the left-hand side of this equation are added up, there are four atoms—two atoms of hydrogen and two atoms of oxygen. But on the right-hand side, there are three atoms—two atoms of hydrogen and one of oxygen.

To fix this, the equation needs to be balanced. The balanced chemical equation for the formation of water looks like this:

$$2\ H_2 + O_2 \rightarrow 2\ H_2O$$

The number 2 in front of the joined hydrogen atoms on the reactant side of this chemical equation shows how many of these joined diatomic molecules are necessary for the chemical reaction to take place. The number 2 is written on the line and in front of the chemical symbol because the two pairs of hydrogen atoms are not chemically joined.

In order for this chemical reaction to take place, two pairs of hydrogen atoms are needed to react with one pair of oxygen atoms. Notice that there is not a number 1 written in front of the two joined oxygen atoms, since there is only one atom. Therefore, the number 1 is just assumed to be there.

Now if the numbers of atoms in this chemical equation are added up, there is the same number of hydrogen atoms and oxygen atoms on both sides of the equation:

$2\ H_2$	+	O_2	$\rightarrow$	$2\ H_2O$
4 H atoms	+	2 O atoms		4 H atoms and 2 O atoms

No atoms have been created or destroyed: They have just been rearranged. This balanced chemical equation would tell a chemist that if two hydrogen molecules and one oxygen molecule react together, they will always make two water molecules.

Because matter cannot be created or destroyed in a chemical reaction, the mass of all of the reactants will always add up to the total mass of all of the products. This is called the ***law of conservation of mass***.

Chemical reactions make new substances by taking the atoms that already exist in the reactants and rearranging them into different combinations to form the products—no new element can suddenly be created. For instance, in the earlier example, where hydrogen reacts with oxygen, carbon dioxide (CO_2) could never be a product of the reaction, because carbon is not one of the reactants. If an element is not present in the reactants, it will never appear in the products of a chemical reaction.

In order to end up with an element that was not in the reactants, the particles in the nucleus of an atom—the protons and neutrons—would have to change. This is a different type of reaction, called a **nuclear reaction**. Some nuclear reactions occur naturally in elements that are described as **radioactive**. The nuclei of radioactive elements are unstable. Since they are unstable, they can fall apart and give off subatomic particles. Eventually, through a process called ***radioactive decay***, these unstable elements are transformed into a stable (nonradioactive) element. When an atom of one element is changed into an atom of another element through a nuclear reaction, it is called ***transmutation***.

Radioactive decay is one way in which transmutations occur. Other types of transmutations are **fission** and **fusion**. Nuclear fission occurs when the nucleus of an element splits into smaller pieces. Fusion, on the other hand, is when two nuclei combine to produce a larger nucleus. These reactions give off an enormous amount of energy.

The rest of this book is dedicated to the discussion of chemical reactions, not nuclear reactions. Chemical reactions are the ones that create and break chemical bonds to form new substances. They do not change the composition of the nucleus of any of

NUCLEAR ENERGY

Nuclear reactions are quite different from chemical reactions. In chemical reactions, electrons outside the nucleus interact to form chemical bonds. In nuclear reactions, protons and neutrons react inside the nucleus and form elements that were not present in the reactants.

There are two types of nuclear reactions: fission and fusion. In a fusion reaction, the nuclei of two atoms "fuse" to make a larger nucleus. Since the number of protons is different, this creates a different element.

Fusion is what powers the Sun and stars. One type of fusion reaction involves the combination of two "heavy" isotopes of hydrogen. Isotopes of an element have the same number of protons, but a different number of neutrons. For example, hydrogen and its isotopes—deuterium and tritium—all have one proton in their nuclei. Remember that the number of protons plus the number of neutrons make up the mass of an atom. Because they have different numbers of neutrons, hydrogen, deuterium, and tritium have different masses. Deuterium has one proton and one neutron. It has a mass of 2 atomic mass units (amu). Deuterium can also be written as hydrogen-2. The number following the element's name is the isotope's mass. Tritium has one proton and two neutrons. So, tritium has a mass of 3 amu. Tritium can be written as hydrogen-3.

When a deuterium isotope and a tritium isotope fuse, they create the element helium, plus an extra neutron. Here is what the reaction looks like:

$$^{2}_{1}H + ^{3}_{1}H \rightarrow ^{4}_{2}He + ^{1}_{0}n$$

the atoms involved in the chemical reaction. The next chapter will explain how chemical bonds form when atoms give, take, or share electrons.

The first symbol represents deuterium. The number 1 below the line is the number of protons. The number 2 above the line shows the mass of the isotope. The other reactant is tritium. When the nuclei fuse, there are now two protons. The only element that has two protons is helium. Since the number of protons and the masses on both sides of nuclear reactions must be equal, that leaves one subatomic particle with a mass of 1 amu and no charge—a neutron.

Fusion reactions, or thermonuclear reactions, release amazing amounts of energy. Inside stars and the Sun, hydrogen atoms are constantly undergoing fusion reactions and giving off energy that we see as light and feel as heat.

Fission, on the other hand, is the splitting of a nucleus into parts. This also gives off a lot of energy. Most nuclear power plants in use today use fission reactions, which are easier to contain within the power plant—and therefore are safer—than fusion reactions. Nuclear fission occurs when isotopes of certain elements are hit with neutrons. The following reaction shows what happens to uranium-235 when a neutron hits it.

$$^{235}_{92}U + ^{1}_{0}n \rightarrow ^{236}_{92}U \rightarrow ^{142}_{56}Ba + ^{91}_{36}Kr + ^{1}_{0}n + ^{1}_{0}n + ^{1}_{0}n$$

First, the uranium-235 changes into uranium-236, a very unstable isotope. Then, the uranium-236 undergoes fission, breaking apart and producing two daughter atoms—barium-142 and krypton-91, plus several neutrons. In a nuclear power plant, the heat generated during these reactions is captured and used to produce electricity.

Chemical Bonding

Chemical reactions rearrange the elements in the reactants to form different groupings of those same elements in the new products. The products of a chemical reaction can be any combination of compounds, molecules, or elements. For example, when iron (Fe) reacts with the oxygen (O_2) in the air to form rust (Fe_2O_3), the two elements that are the reactants form one new compound that includes both elements:

4 Fe	+	3 O_2	→	2 Fe_2O_3
element		diatomic element		new compound

When methane (CH_4), a major component in natural gas, is burned to produce energy, the products are carbon dioxide (CO_2) and water:

CH_4	+	$2\ O_2$	→	CO_2	+	$2\ H_2O$
compound		molecule (or diatomic element)		new compound		new compound

When pieces of zinc (Zn) are dropped into sulfuric acid (H_2SO_4), bubbles of hydrogen gas appear and a new compound, zinc sulfate ($ZnSO_4$), is formed:

Zn	+	H_2SO_4	→	$ZnSO_4$	+	H_2
element		compound		different compound		diatomic element

Compounds and molecules, such as the ones above, are groups of two or more elements that are held together by a chemical bond. Since the atoms in the products of a chemical reaction are rearranged, they are different chemicals and they behave differently than the reactants do.

For example, look at the formation of sodium chloride (NaCl) from its elements, sodium (Na) and chlorine (Cl_2):

2 Na	+	Cl_2	→	2 NaCl
element		diatomic element		new compound

Sodium is a silver-colored metal that reacts violently with water. Even the humidity in the air can make sodium burst into flames. As a precaution, pure sodium metal is often stored in oil to keep the water in the air from getting to its surface. Chlorine, on the other hand, is a pale, greenish-colored gas that is so poisonous it was used as a chemical weapon in World War I. When it is inhaled, chlorine gas causes chest pains and a burning sensation in the throat. It can destroy lung tissue and victims die of suffocation because they cannot breathe.

Figure 3.1 The product of a chemical reaction can be quite different from its "parent" elements. a) Sodium is a soft metal that is highly reactive with water. b) Chlorine is a toxic gas. c) The highly reactive sodium and dangerously toxic chlorine, when combined, create a perfectly harmless addition to any kitchen: table salt.

But when sodium metal and chlorine gas react with one another, the product is neither flammable nor poisonous. The reaction of these two chemicals makes sodium chloride, or ordinary table salt. Even though table salt has sodium and chlorine atoms in it, its chemical properties are very different than the chemical properties of either of its parent elements. That is because the atoms of the two very different elements have formed a compound that is now held together by chemical bonds in an arrangement that gives the compound unique chemical properties.

THE ATOM AND ITS STRUCTURE

An understanding of the structure of the smallest particle of matter, the atom, is very important to understanding how chemical bonds form. Remember that inside the nucleus of the atom, there are subatomic particles called *protons* and *neutrons*. Orbiting the nucleus is another type of subatomic particle, called *electrons*. Electrons are the parts of the atom that take part in chemical bonding. Chemical bonds occur when atoms gain, lose, or share electrons. Chemical reactions happen when these chemical bonds are formed or when they are broken.

Electrons move around the nucleus of an atom in **energy levels**, which are sometimes called *shells* or *orbitals*. The energy level of an electron is the area around the nucleus where the electron is most likely to be found. The energy level that is closest to the atom's nucleus is called the *first energy level*. The farther an electron gets from the nucleus, the higher the energy level it is on.

According to an early theory about the atom, the atom looks like a mini solar system. The nucleus of the atom would be the "Sun" and the electrons are the orbiting "planets." This model of the atom is called the ***Bohr model***. It is named for the Danish physicist, Niels Bohr, who proposed electron shells in 1913. The Bohr model is very useful for understanding how atoms work, but it does not answer some questions about the behavior of all atoms.

So, a new model was proposed and accepted. The modern description of how electrons move around the nucleus in an atom is called the ***quantum mechanical model***. In this model, the electrons do not follow an exact path, or "orbit," around the nucleus the way they do in Bohr's model. Instead, for the new model, physicists calculated the chance of finding an electron in a certain position at any given time. The quantum mechanical model looks like a fuzzy

CARBON-14 DATING

One type of nuclear reaction can help scientists figure out the age of certain artifacts, such as dinosaur bones, mummies, or wooden tools left behind by ancient people. This technique, called *carbon-14 dating*, can be used on any organic material. Organic materials are things that are living or were once living.

Carbon-14 is a natural isotope of carbon. It is also a radioisotope, which means that it is radioactive. Radioisotopes break down, or decay, in a specific amount of time. The amount of time it takes for half of the atoms of a radioisotope to decay is called its *half-life*. The half-life of carbon-14 is about 5,700 years.

Scientists use this fact to help them date artifacts. Of all of the carbon atoms in the universe, about 1 in 1 trillion of them are carbon-14 atoms. Carbon-14 exists naturally in the atmosphere, mostly in the form of carbon dioxide (CO_2). Some carbon dioxide molecules contain carbon-14 instead of carbon-12.

Carbon dioxide molecules get absorbed by plants and are used during a process called *photosynthesis*. Some of the carbon dioxide absorbed by the plants will contain carbon-12 atoms, while other carbon dioxide molecules will contain carbon-14 atoms. Since humans and animals eat plants, their bodies also contain some carbon-12 and some carbon-14.

In fact, the ratio of carbon-12 atoms to carbon-14 atoms in all living things is basically constant. Even though the carbon-14 atoms decay, these atoms are

cloud. The cloud is the most dense where the chance of finding an electron is high. It is less dense where the chance is low. The newer model is more difficult to visualize than Bohr's model, though, so for simplicity's sake the older Bohr model will be used for the rest of the discussion of energy levels.

Remember that the nucleus of an atom is positively charged because it contains protons and neutrons. The protons have a

constantly being replaced. At this moment, every living thing contains a certain percentage of carbon-14 atoms. But as soon as an organism dies, it stops taking in new carbon atoms.

At death, the ratio of carbon-12 atoms to carbon-14 atoms is the same as all other living things. But as the carbon-14 atoms decay, those atoms are not replaced. So, the ratio of carbon-12 to carbon-14 starts to change. By determining the ratio of carbon-12 to carbon-14 in the deceased organism, and comparing it to the ratio in organisms that are still alive, scientists can figure out how long an organism has been dead.

For example, say a paleontologist finds two mummies. The scientist determines that one mummy contains half of the carbon-14 that organisms alive today have. The other mummy has 25% of the carbon-14 that a living organism has. From this information, the paleontologist knows that the first mummy must be about 5,700 years old, while the second one is around 11,400 years old. Using the knowledge that a half-life means that half of the carbon-14 has already decayed, here is a sample of what the scientist's calculations might have looked like in order to determine the age of the mummies:

Mummy #1—50% carbon-14 = ½ carbon-14 = 1 half-life = 5,700 years old
Mummy #2—25% carbon-14 = ¼ carbon-14 = 2 half-lives = 11,400 years old

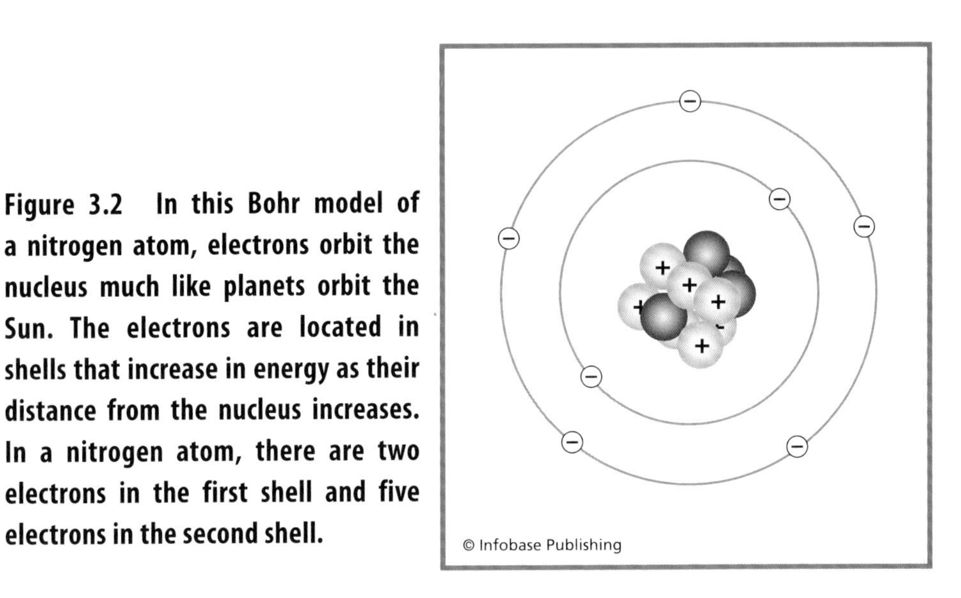

Figure 3.2 In this Bohr model of a nitrogen atom, electrons orbit the nucleus much like planets orbit the Sun. The electrons are located in shells that increase in energy as their distance from the nucleus increases. In a nitrogen atom, there are two electrons in the first shell and five electrons in the second shell.

positive charge and the neutrons are neutral and have no charge at all. The electrons have a negative charge. Since opposite charges attract one another (think of a magnet), electrons are attracted to the nucleus. Electrons can move from one energy level to another if they gain or lose just the right amount of energy. It is easier for some electrons to move than it is for others because the electrons in higher energy levels are farther away from the nucleus and its attractive force. So, electrons in the outermost energy levels need less energy to break away from the nucleus.

These electrons in the highest energy level are called ***valence electrons***. In 1916, American chemist Gilbert Newton Lewis observed that elements are most stable when they have eight electrons in their highest energy level. In fact, all of the **noble gases**, which are the most chemically inactive (or **inert**) elements known, have eight electrons in their highest energy levels (except for helium which has only two). Lewis proposed that elements form chemical bonds with one another in order to fill their highest energy level with eight electrons. His idea is called the ***octet rule*** (the prefix *oct-* means "eight").

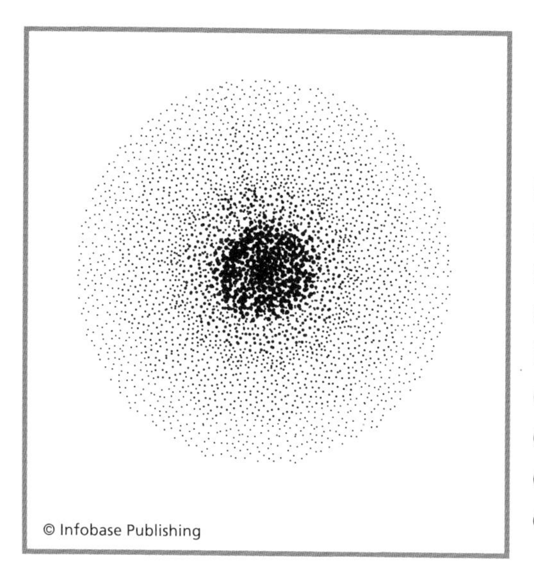

Figure 3.3 The quantum mechanical model states that individual electrons do not orbit around the nucleus in exact paths but instead are located in an "electron cloud." The electron cloud indicates the probable location of an electron at a given moment. The darker the area, the more likely an electron will be found there.

When an atom's outermost electron shell is full of electrons, that atom is stable. In other words, it is inert, or chemically inactive. In order to get a full outermost electron shell, atoms will gain, lose, or share their valence electrons. This gaining, losing, or sharing of electrons is what makes a chemical bond.

IONIC BONDS

Sodium has one valence electron in its outermost electron shell. Chlorine has seven. If a sodium atom gives its one valence electron to the chlorine atom, the chlorine atom will have eight valence electrons. By giving up the one electron on its outermost shell, sodium loses that empty shell. Now sodium's outermost shell contains eight electrons, too.

Remember that in a neutral atom, the number of protons in the nucleus equals the number of electrons moving around the nucleus. Since protons have a positive charge and electrons have a negative charge, the atom is neutral when their numbers are equal. When sodium gives up an electron, though, the atom now has one more proton than its number of electrons. This gives the sodium a positive charge. This is called a *sodium* ***ion***. An ion is any atom or group of atoms with an electric charge. The charge can be positive, resulting from the loss of electrons, such as in the sodium ion, or the charge can be negative if the ion gains electrons. The chlorine atom, for example, has gained an electron and now has one more electron than proton. Since electrons have negative charges, the chlorine now has a negative charge and it is a chlorine ion.

When two or more ions bond together chemically, it is called an ***ionic bond***. In an ionic bond, the ions are attracted to one another because they have opposite charges. In general, ionic bonds form between a **metal** and a **nonmetal**. Since sodium is a metal and chlorine is a nonmetal, when they bond, an ionic bond is formed and sodium chloride is produced.

Metals are elements that are **malleable**, **ductile**, **lustrous,** and good conductors of heat and electricity. Malleability is a physical property of metals. It means that they can be hammered, pounded, or bent into different shapes without breaking. Ductility is similar, but it specifically means that metals can be shaped, or drawn, into wires. Metals are also **lustrous**, which means they are glossy or shiny. In addition, heat and electricity flow through metals easily,

HELIUM AND THE OCTET RULE

Helium does not have eight electrons in its highest energy level because it only has one energy level. This first energy level can only hold two electrons and then it is full. Since helium only has two electrons, its highest energy level contains the most electrons it can hold. That is why helium is still considered a noble gas and why it is, essentially, inert.

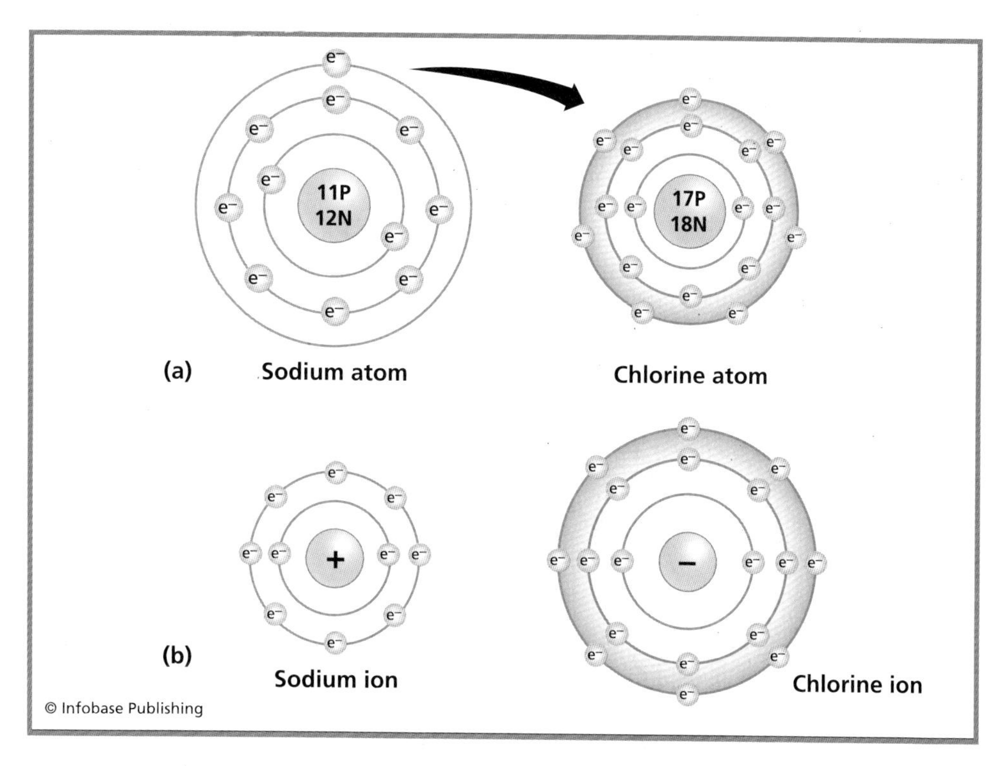

Figure 3.4 a) A sodium atom donates its one valence electron to a chlorine atom. b) As a result, both atoms have eight electrons in their outermost shells.

so they are good conductors. With the exception of mercury, all the metallic elements are solids at room temperature. Mercury, which is sometimes used in thermometers, is a liquid at room temperature. A majority of the known elements are metals.

Nonmetals, on the other hand, are not good conductors of heat or electricity. They are not lustrous, either. Some nonmetals are solids at room temperature, but others are gases or liquids. Most of the nonmetals are grouped on the right-hand side of the periodic table. The only exception to this rule is hydrogen, which is a

WATER SOFTENING

Sometimes people refer to water as being "hard" or "soft." If someone says water is hard, he means that there are a lot of calcium (Ca^{2+}) or magnesium (Mg^{2+}) ions dissolved in it. Hard water causes several problems. First, it can cause scales to form on the inside of pipes, water heaters, or teakettles. These scales occur when the calcium or magnesium precipitates out of solution and sticks to the insides of pipes. The scales build up and eventually the pipes are completely clogged. Hard water also prevents soap from lathering, and it reacts with soap to leave behind a sticky film commonly called *soap scum*.

There are two solutions to soften water that is too hard. First, the water could be filtered to remove all of the calcium and magnesium ions. But this can be very expensive, so most people use a water softener instead. A water softener is a piece of equipment that can be attached to the water pipes that run into a house. This way, all the household water goes through the water softener before going into the other pipes in the house. Inside a water softener are small plastic beads. These beads have sodium ions (Na^{+}) stuck on them. As the water flows over the bed of beads, the magnesium and calcium ions get replaced with the sodium ions. Since sodium is easily dissolved in water, it does not precipitate out in pipes like calcium and magnesium ions do. As a result, no scales form inside the pipes. Sodium ions do not react with soap to form soap scum, either, and they allow the soap to lather properly.

Eventually, though, all the sodium ions inside the water softener will be replaced with magnesium or calcium ions. When this happens, the water softener has to be recharged. To do this, a very salty saltwater solution, called *brine*, is flushed through the water softener. The sodium ions in the salt water replace the magnesium or calcium ions and the water softener is ready to go again.

nonmetal found in Group 1 on the left-hand side of the periodic table. Hydrogen was placed in Group 1 because it shares many chemical properties with the other elements in Group 1.

COVALENT BONDS

Giving away and taking in electrons are not the only ways in which atoms can get eight electrons in their outermost electron shell. They can also share electrons. The oxygen and hydrogen in water do this. When atoms share electrons, it is called a ***covalent bond***. Covalent bonds most often happen between two or more nonmetals.

Take the case of hydrogen and oxygen joining to form water: Oxygen needs two electrons to fill up its outermost electron shell. But hydrogen does not give up its valance electron as easily as sodium does. Rather than give away its only electron, the hydrogen

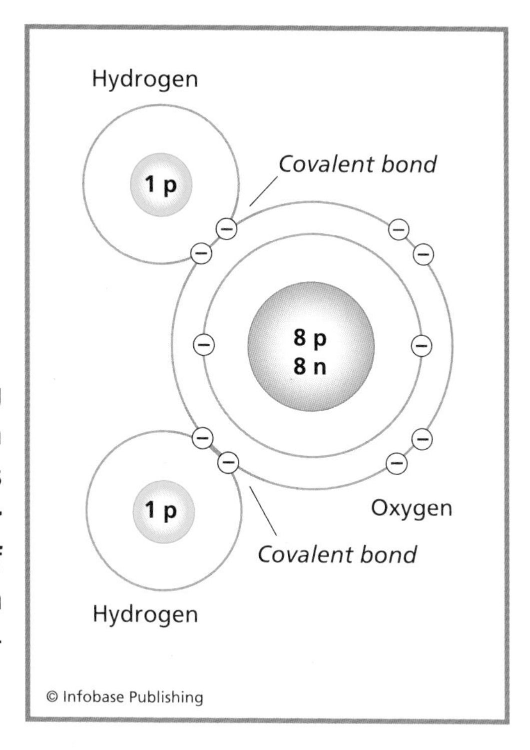

Figure 3.5 The sharing of electrons between two atoms is known as a covalent bond. Water (H_2O) is an example of a molecule in which the atoms form covalent bonds.

atom will share it. So, two hydrogen atoms will share their electrons with one oxygen atom. This is why water's chemical formula is H_2O. With the hydrogen atoms sharing their electrons, the oxygen atom now has eight electrons in its outermost shell, making it stable. Each hydrogen atom gets an electron to share, giving it two electrons on its outermost electron shell. Hydrogen, like helium, only has one energy level, which can hold a maximum of two electrons. When the hydrogen shares an electron with oxygen, its outermost energy level is full and it is stable.

All this giving up, taking in, and sharing of electrons are the ways in which atoms are rearranged to form different chemical compounds and molecules when they react during chemical reactions. There are many types of chemical reactions. Chemists classify them according to certain patterns.

Types of Chemical Reactions

The only way to be absolutely certain of the products that are produced by a chemical reaction is to carry out the reaction in a laboratory and analyze the chemicals that result. There are millions of known chemical compounds, and all of these compounds can be combined in many different ways in order to produce different chemical reactions. As a result, it would be impossible to conduct and analyze every chemical reaction in a laboratory. Instead, chemists have studied chemical reactions and determined that many of them follow a predictable pattern. Using these patterns allows chemists to predict the products in many chemical reactions, even if they do not have the time or the money to carry them out in a laboratory.

SYNTHESIS REACTIONS

One type of chemical reaction is the **synthesis reaction**. The word *synthesis* means "to put together." A synthesis reaction involves a reaction between, or among, two or more elements, molecules, or compounds. There is only one product in a synthesis reaction. Synthesis reactions can also be called ***combination reactions***. The reaction between hydrogen and oxygen to form water is an example of a synthesis reaction:

$2\ H_2$	+	O_2	→	$2\ H_2O$
element		element		one product

Here is another example of a synthesis reaction. This time, the reactants are compounds:

SO_2	+	H_2O	→	H_2SO_3
compound		compound		one product

A reaction with only one product is probably a synthesis (combination) reaction.

DECOMPOSITION REACTIONS

To *decompose* means "to break apart." In a **decomposition reaction**, one reactant breaks apart and forms two or more products. When electricity is passed through water, the water will break down, or decompose, and produce hydrogen and oxygen. The chemical equation for this reaction is the opposite of the synthesis reaction that makes water:

$2\ H_2O$	→	$2\ H_2$	+	O_2
one reactant		element		element

The reaction that produces lime from limestone is a decomposition reaction, too. Limestone is a type of rock that is made up mostly of the chemical compound calcium carbonate ($CaCO_3$). When calcium carbonate is heated, it decomposes into calcium oxide (CaO) and carbon dioxide. Calcium oxide is commonly known as lime. Many people add lime to their garden soil if the soil is too acidic to grow their vegetables:

$CaCO_3$	→	CaO	+	CO_2
one reactant		compound		compound

A reaction with only one reactant and two or more products is probably a decomposition reaction.

SINGLE DISPLACEMENT REACTIONS

In a **single displacement reaction**, one element switches places with another element in a compound. The reactants in a single displacement reaction are an element and a compound, and the products are a different element and a different compound. A single displacement reaction can also be called a ***single replacement reaction***. Look at this example of a single displacement reaction:

Zn	+	2 HCl	→	$ZnCl_2$	+	H_2
element		compound		different compound		different (diatomic) element

In this reaction, the element zinc (Zn) takes the place of hydrogen in the compound hydrochloric acid (HCl). When the zinc and hydrogen switch places, the products are zinc chloride ($ZnCl_2$) and hydrogen gas (H_2).

Not every element will take the place of another element in a compound, though. Whether the reaction will take place or not depends on the activity of the two elements. For metals, there is a list called the ***activity series of metals*** that lists the metals in order of decreasing reactivity. Any metal that is higher on the list will replace any metal listed below it in the activity series. Since hydrogen is below zinc, the zinc will take hydrogen's place in the hydrochloric acid and the reaction will occur as shown in the earlier chemical equation.

Here is another example:

Al	+	$3\ AgNO_3$	→	$Al(NO_3)_3$	+	$3\ Ag$
element		compound		different compound		different element

In this reaction, the aluminum (Al) will take the place of silver (Ag) in the compound silver nitrate ($AgNO_3$) because aluminum is more reactive, and, therefore, above silver in the activity series.

But if a chemist placed metallic silver into hydrochloric acid, nothing would happen. That is because silver is not as reactive as hydrogen. It is below hydrogen in the activity series and it cannot replace the hydrogen in the reaction:

Ag	+	$2\ HCl$	→	no reaction;
element		compound		silver cannot take the place of hydrogen

Many metals, such as zinc, iron, lead, copper, and aluminum are found chemically bonded to oxygen in nature. Sometimes, chemists can use single displacement reactions to get the pure metal.

Some nonmetals can replace another nonmetal from a compound, too. This replacement is usually limited to the nonmetals called the ***halogens*** (fluorine, chlorine, bromine, and iodine). The halogens can be found in Group 17 on the periodic table. The activity of the halogens decreases as you go down Group 17. Fluorine is the most active and iodine is the least.

Activity Series

Metal	Oxidation Reaction			
Lithium	$Li(s) \longrightarrow$	$Li^{+}(aq)$	+	e^{-}
Potassium	$K(s) \longrightarrow$	$K^{+}(aq)$	+	e^{-}
Barium	$Ba(s) \longrightarrow$	$Ba^{2+}(aq)$	+	$2e^{-}$
Calcium	$Ca(s) \longrightarrow$	$Ca^{2+}(aq)$	+	$2e^{-}$
Sodium	$Na(s) \longrightarrow$	$Na^{+}(aq)$	+	e^{-}
Magnesium	$Mg(s) \longrightarrow$	$Mg^{2+}(aq)$	+	$2e^{-}$
Aluminum	$Al(s) \longrightarrow$	$Al^{3+}(aq)$	+	$3e^{-}$
Manganese	$Mn(s) \longrightarrow$	$Mn^{2+}(aq)$	+	$2e^{-}$
Zinc	$Zn(s) \longrightarrow$	$Zn^{2+}(aq)$	+	$2e^{-}$
Chromium	$Cr(s) \longrightarrow$	$Cr^{3+}(aq)$	+	$3e^{-}$
Iron	$Fe(s) \longrightarrow$	$Fe^{2+}(aq)$	+	$2e^{-}$
Cobalt	$Co(s) \longrightarrow$	$Co^{2+}(aq)$	+	$2e^{-}$
Nickel	$Ni(s) \longrightarrow$	$Ni^{2+}(aq)$	+	$2e^{-}$
Tin	$Sn(s) \longrightarrow$	$Sn^{2+}(aq)$	+	$2e^{-}$
Lead	$Pb(s) \longrightarrow$	$Pb^{2+}(aq)$	+	$2e^{-}$
Hydrogen	$H_2(g) \longrightarrow$	$2H^{+}(aq)$	+	$2e^{-}$
Copper	$Cu(s) \longrightarrow$	$Cu^{2+}(aq)$	+	$2e^{-}$
Silver	$Ag(s) \longrightarrow$	$Ag^{+}(aq)$	+	e^{-}
Mercury	$Hg(l) \longrightarrow$	$Hg^{2+}(aq)$	+	$2e^{-}$
Platinum	$Pt(s) \longrightarrow$	$Pt^{2+}(aq)$	+	$2e^{-}$
Gold	$Au(s) \longrightarrow$	$Au^{3+}(aq)$	+	$3e^{-}$

Ease of oxidation increases

Figure 4.1 The activity series indicates how easily metals can be oxidized. Metals at the top of the list are more likely to oxidize (give up electrons) than metals at the bottom of the list.

In the following reaction, the chlorine (Cl) replaces the iodine (I) in the compound potassium iodide (KI) because chlorine is more active:

Cl_2	+	2 KI	→	2 KCl	+	I_2
element		compound		different compound		different element

On the other hand, a reaction between bromine (Br_2) and sodium chloride (NaCl), will not occur:

Br_2	+	NaCl	→	no reaction;
element		compound		bromine cannot take the place of chlorine

No reaction occurs because bromine is not active enough to replace the chlorine in the compound.

DOUBLE DISPLACEMENT REACTIONS

In a **double displacement reaction**, atoms from two different compounds switch places. The reactants are two compounds and the products are two different compounds. Double displacement reactions can also be called ***double replacement reactions***. Here is an example of a double displacement reaction:

Fe_2O_3	+	6 HCl	→	2 $FeCl_3$	+	3 H_2O
compound		compound		different compound		different compound

Fe is the chemical symbol for iron. It comes from iron's Latin name, *Ferrum*. In this reaction, the iron in iron oxide (Fe_2O_3) switches places with the hydrogen in the hydrochloric acid (HCl). Double displacement reactions are like two pairs of dancers switching partners.

Many double displacement reactions occur between ionic compounds that are dissolved in water. Sometimes one of the products of a double displacement reaction will come out of **solution**, usually as a gas or a precipitate. Solutions are mixtures of two or more substances, called the **solutes**, dissolved in another substance, the **solvent**. For example, salt water is a solution. The salt is the solute and the water is the solvent. In a solution, it is impossible to see the separate parts. But if two chemicals that are dissolved in water

VITAMINS IN DARK GLASSES

Ever wonder why some vitamin supplements are stored in dark or opaque bottles? It is not because the pharmacist thought that these bottles looked nicer. It is because some vitamins break down in the presence of light. Light is a form of energy, and when some vitamins absorb light, that energy can start a chemical reaction. These reactions are called *light-induced chemical reactions*. Vitamin A, vitamin B12, vitamin D, folic acid, vitamin K, vitamin E, and riboflavin can all be affected by chemical reactions caused by light. Because of this, they need to be kept in dark or opaque bottles.

Vitamins are not the only things that can break down in the presence of light. In fact, in the presence of oxygen, moisture, and temperature changes—or, even worse, all three—light can trigger chemical reactions that will break down paper, cloth, and ink. If enough light energy is absorbed, the paper, cloth, or ink can be irreversibly damaged. Art historians must be on the lookout for these chemical reactions every day.

Light-induced chemical reactions can also affect milk. Not only can the vitamins in the milk be broken down if the milk is exposed to light, but the milk can also develop an off-flavor. That happens because light can cause the amino acids and proteins in milk to break down. The clearer the milk container, the faster the milk loses quality. Clear glass is the worst container for milk. Plastic jugs will not let as much light in as a glass container, but for the best tasting milk that is full of vitamins, cardboard cartons are the best.

react chemically, the product could be something that will not dissolve in water. That product, then, will no longer be in a solution. Substances that will not dissolve are called ***insoluble***. If the insoluble product is a gas, the gas will bubble out of the solution, in the same way carbon dioxide gas bubbles out of soda when a bottle of soda is opened. If the insoluble product is a solid, the solid will fall out of the solution as a precipitate.

$2\ NaCN\ (aq)$	+	$H_2SO_4\ (aq)$	→	$2\ HCN\ (g)$	+	$Na_2SO_4\ (aq)$
compound		compound		different compound		different compound

In the double displacement reaction above, dissolved sodium cyanide (NaCN) and sulfuric acid (H_2SO_4) react to form sodium sulfate (Na_2SO_4) and an extremely poisonous gas called *hydrogen cyanide* (HCN). The (aq) means these substances are an **aqueous solution**. An aqueous solution is made by dissolving chemicals in water. In this reaction, the sodium cyanide, sulfuric acid, and sodium sulfate are all dissolved in water. The (g) that follows the formula for hydrogen cyanide indicates that this chemical is a gas. The hydrogen cyanide will bubble out of the solution, leaving behind the sodium sulfate that is still dissolved in the water.

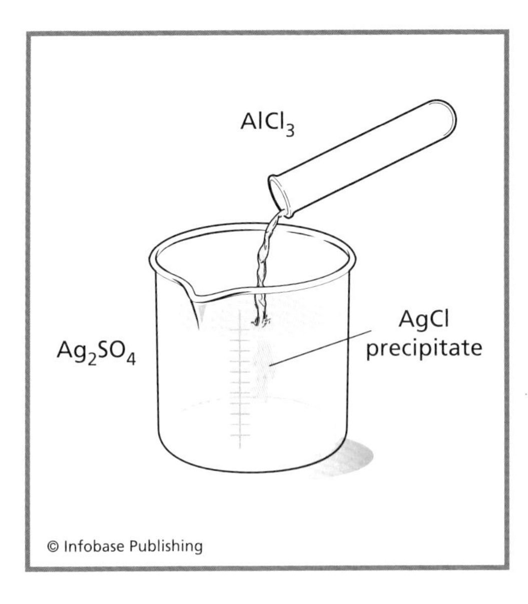

Figure 4.2 The mixing of a silver sulfate solution with an aluminum chloride solution, results in the formation of aqueous aluminum sulfate and the precipitation of silver chloride. This is an example of a double displacement reaction.

In the example of a double displacement reaction below, a silver sulfate (Ag_2SO_4) solution is mixed with an aluminum chloride ($AlCl_3$) solution. One of the products, silver chloride (AgCl), precipitates out of the solution as a solid. The (s) following the formula for silver chloride shows that it is a solid.

$3\ Ag_2SO_4\ (aq)$	+	$2\ AlCl_3\ (aq)$	→	$6\ AgCl\ (s)$	+	$Al_2(SO_4)_3\ (aq)$
compound		compound		different compound		different compound

COMBUSTION REACTIONS

Combustion is what people commonly call "burning." In a combustion reaction, oxygen is always one of the reactants. If the oxygen is removed, the reaction stops. (This is why firefighters use a variety of methods to cut off the oxygen supply to a fire.) In a combustion reaction, some type of **hydrocarbon** is usually one of the other reactants. Hydrocarbons are chemical compounds that are made up of hydrogen and carbon. Wood, gasoline, and alcohol are all examples of hydrocarbons. Hydrocarbons are not the only things that burn, though. Some metals will also combust in the presence of oxygen.

Any chemical reaction that gives off heat is called an ***exothermic reaction***. Combustion reactions are always exothermic because they always give off heat. Sometimes they give off light, too. For example, wood burning in a fireplace is an exothermic combustion reaction, giving off both light and heat.

Endothermic reactions are chemical reactions that need to absorb energy in order to occur. Cooking pasta is an example of an endothermic reaction. As long as the pasta gets energy from the boiling water, it will cook. If the pasta is taken out of the hot water and rinsed in cold water, it stops cooking right away. An endothermic reaction will stop if the energy that drives it is taken away.

There are two types of combustion reactions: a **complete combustion** and an **incomplete combustion**. The products of the complete combustion of a hydrocarbon—carbon dioxide and water vapor (steam)—are both gases. For example, if propane (C_3H_8) is burned in the presence of pure oxygen, the products will be carbon dioxide and water:

$$\underset{\text{hydrocarbon}}{C_3H_8} + \underset{\text{oxygen}}{5\,O_2} \rightarrow \underset{\text{carbon dioxide}}{3\,CO_2} + \underset{\text{water}}{4\,H_2O} + \underset{\text{energy}}{\text{heat}}$$

Incomplete combustion will occur if there is not enough oxygen for the reaction to continue. This is much more common than complete combustion. Unlike complete combustion reactions, incomplete combustion reactions result in other products besides carbon dioxide and water. The byproducts of incomplete combustion reactions can include soot, which is elemental carbon (C). Other byproducts include nitrous oxides, sulfur oxides, and deadly carbon monoxide.

For example, octane (C_8H_{18}) is the main ingredient of gasoline. When gasoline burns in a car, the products are carbon dioxide (CO_2), carbon monoxide (CO), water vapor (H_2O), and nitrous oxide (NO).

$$2\,C_8H_{18} + 25\,O_2 + 2\,N_2 \rightarrow 12\,CO_2 + 4\,CO + 4\,NO + 18\,H_2O + \text{heat}$$

Gasoline needs oxygen in order to burn. The oxygen comes from air that is drawn into the car and mixed with the gasoline. Gasoline needs nitrogen (N_2), too, which also comes from the air. (Earth's atmosphere is 78% nitrogen.)

Combustion reactions are needed to heat homes and run cars. Since most of these reactions involve incomplete combustion, they should always take place in well-ventilated areas. Carbon monoxide (CO) can be deadly. And soot (C), nitrogen oxides (N_xO_x), and sulfur oxides (S_xO_x) are all pollutants that can harm health and the environment.

ACID-BASE REACTIONS

Acid-base reactions are a special type of double displacement reaction. Acid-base reactions occur when an **acid** and a **base** react with one another. An acid is a compound that contains hydrogen and gives off hydrogen ions (H^+) when it is dissolved in water. Bases, on the other hand, produce hydroxide ions (OH^-) when they are dissolved in water.

Many common household items contain acids. For example, vinegar, tomatoes, citrus fruits, and carbonated sodas all have acids in them. All vinegars contain acetic acid ($HC_2H_3O_2$), also known as ethanoic acid. Tomatoes contain ascorbic acid ($HC_6H_7O_6$), citrus fruits have citric acid ($HC_6H_7O_7$) in them, and many carbonated beverages contain phosphoric acid (H_3PO_4). These acids give these foods, and many others, a tart or sour taste.

Milk of magnesia, which can be taken as an antacid medicine, is a base. The chemical name for milk of magnesia is magnesium hydroxide ($Mg(OH)_2$). Magnesium hydroxide can ease the discomfort caused by too much stomach acid. Potassium hydroxide (KOH) and sodium hydroxide (NaOH) are also bases. These chemicals, sometimes called *lye*, and are used in making soap. Sodium hydroxide is also an ingredient of oven and drain cleaners. Bases feel slippery and have a bitter taste.

Because an acid is a compound that produces hydrogen ions (H^+) when it is dissolved in water and a base produces hydroxide (OH^-) ions, when acids and bases react with one another, they produce water and an **ionic salt**. For example, when hydrochloric acid (HCl) reacts with sodium hydroxide (NaOH), the reaction produces water and sodium chloride, an ionic salt:

HCl	+	NaOH	→	NaCl	+	H_2O
acid		base		an ionic salt		water

Although this reaction actually produces sodium chloride—commonly known as table salt—sodium chloride is not the only ionic salt. Ionic salts are, in fact, defined as compounds that are produced by the combining the **cation** from a base and the **anion** from an acid. A cation is a positive ion and an anion is a negative ion.

Here is another example:

H_2SO_4	+	2 KOH	→	K_2SO_4	+	2 H_2O
sulfuric acid		potassium hydroxide (a base)		potassium sulfate (an ionic salt)		water

In this reaction, the potassium ion (K^+), or cation, from the base combined with the sulfate ion (SO_4^-), or anion. This produced

THE HINDENBURG

On May 6, 1937, the German passenger airship the *Hindenburg* suddenly burst into flames while approaching its landing site in Lakehurst, New Jersey. Thirty-five people out of the 97 on board the airship died in the blaze.

The chemical reaction that took place is the same chemical reaction that produces water.

$$2 H_2 + O_2 \rightarrow 2 H_2O$$

The product of this reaction is harmless, but the combustion of hydrogen is quite explosive. Airships during the 1930s, like the *Hindenburg*, were filled with hydrogen because the gas is lighter than air. Unfortunately, it is also highly flammable.

Today, airships, or blimps, are filled with helium. Helium, like hydrogen, is lighter than air; but unlike hydrogen, helium is a noble gas and is chemically inert, or inactive. The helium does not combust.

the ionic salt known as potassium sulfate (K_2SO_4). The other product—water—results from the combination of hydrogen ions (H^+) produced by the sulfuric acid and hydroxide ions (OH^-) from the potassium hydroxide.

The pH scale is a scale used to determine how acidic or basic a substance is by measuring the number of hydrogen ions in the substance. The pH scale ranges from 0 to 14. A pH of 0 is very acidic, while a very strong base would have a pH value of 14. A neutral solution (a substance that is neither acidic nor basic) would have a pH of 7.

People can use pH indicators to help maintain the correct acid-base balance in a swimming pool, to create soil conditions that are ideal for plant growth, or to make a medical diagnosis. Indicators change colors at different pHs. Some plants are natural pH indicators. Hydrangeas, for example, produce blue flowers in acidic soil, but in basic soils their flowers are pink.

When an acid reacts with a base, it is called a ***neutralization reaction***. The products do not have the same characteristics of either acids or bases. The resulting solutions are neutral:

HCl	+	NaOH	→	NaCl	+	H_2O
acid		base		an ionic salt		water

Like all other acid-base reactions, the reaction that produces table salt and water is a neutralization reaction. In this reaction, both of the reactants are dangerous to work with and are capable of eating through human flesh, but the products are harmless table salt dissolved in water.

OXIDATION-REDUCTION REACTIONS

Combustion reactions are one type of **oxidation reaction**. In the past, the term *oxidation* was used to mean the combination of an element with oxygen to make an oxide. For example, when methane (CH_4) burns in oxygen, it produces oxides of carbon and hydrogen.

ACID RAIN

Under normal conditions, rainwater has a slightly acidic pH of about 5.6. The rainwater becomes acidic because carbon dioxide in the atmosphere combines with the rain to make carbonic acid.

CO_2	+ H_2O	→ H_2CO_3
carbon dioxide	water	carbonic acid

Because carbonic acid is a weak acid, the slightly acidic rain does not usually affect plants or animals. But when rainwater reacts with pollutants such as sulfur oxides (S_xO_x) and nitrogen oxides (N_xO_x), it forms sulfuric acid (H_2SO_4) or sulfurous acid (H_2SO_3) and nitric acid (HNO_3) or nitrous acid (HNO_2). Sulfuric and nitric acids are strong acids. The sulfur and nitrogen oxides in the atmosphere are mainly the result of incomplete combustion in cars and electrical power plants.

Acid rain can kill fish and plants. It can also cause the deterioration of buildings and monuments. Acid rain usually has a pH of around 4, but pHs as low as 2 have been reported in some places. For comparison, vinegar and lemon juice both have a pH of around 2. Rain in the northeastern United States has the lowest pH compared to other areas in the country.

Acid rain tends to have the most noticeable effect in lakes, rivers, and streams where fish are often killed by the abnormally low pH of the water. If one species of fish disappears, the animals that fed on that fish can also disappear because their food is gone. Acid rain can eventually affect entire food chains.

Can anything be done about acid rain damage? Sometimes powdered limestone can be added to lakes and streams affected by acid rain. Limestone is made up mainly of the chemical calcium carbonate ($CaCO_3$). Calcium carbonate is a base and it neutralizes the acid in the water. This process is called *liming*. It is very expensive, and if the acid rain is not stopped, liming is also temporary. The only real way to stop acid rain is to reduce pollution, conserve energy, and find alternative energy sources that do not emit sulfur and nitrogen oxides.

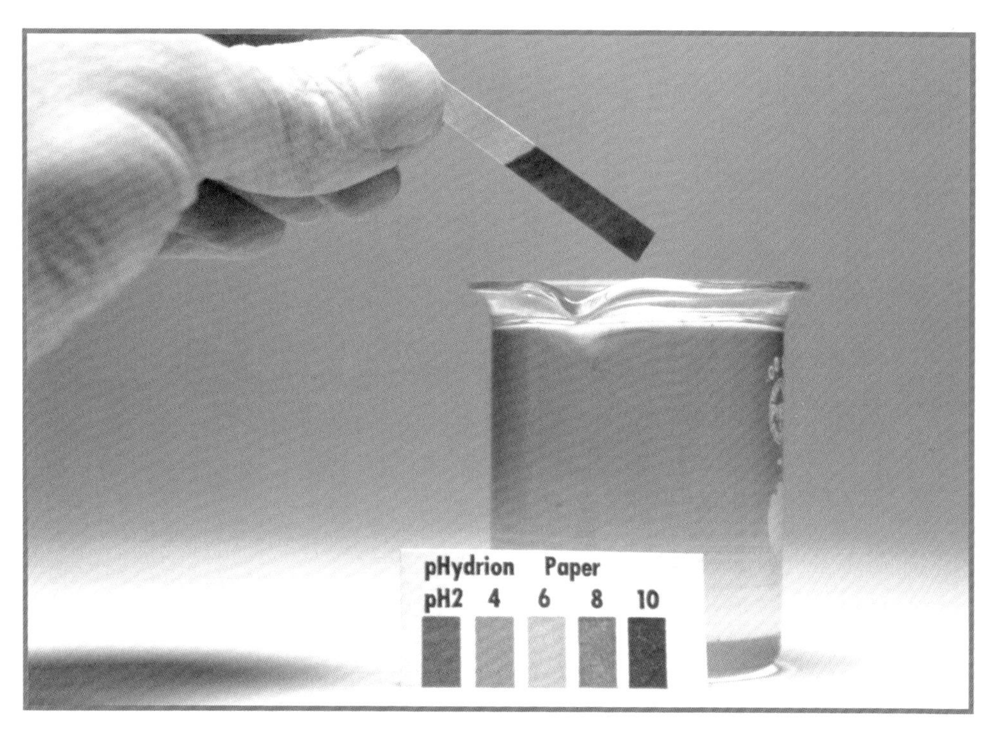

Figure 4.3 To test the basic or acidic qualities of a substance, scientists use a pH indicator. The indicator is a specially treated strip that changes color when placed into the substance. The strip is then compared to a color scale that shows whether the substance is acidic, basic, or neutral in composition.

CH_4	+	$2\ O_2$	→	CO_2	+	$2\ H_2O$
methane		oxygen		carbon di*oxide*		dihydrogen mon*oxide*

Another type of oxidation reaction occurs when iron is exposed to the oxygen in the air. Rust, or iron(III) oxide (Fe_2O_3), is produced. This type of oxidation occurs over a long period of time. The iron does not burn, it just rusts.

$4\ Fe$	+	$3\ O_2$	→	$2\ Fe_2O_3$
iron		oxygen		iron(III) oxide

Today's chemists have expanded the definition of oxidation to be the complete or partial loss of electrons. For example, in the reaction between hydrogen and oxygen to produce water, hydrogen is oxidized:

H_2	+	O_2	→	H_2O
hydrogen		oxygen		dihydrogen mon*oxide*

Both the traditional and modern definitions of oxidation indicate that the hydrogen is oxidized in this reaction. The hydrogen combined with oxygen and produced an oxide. When hydrogen and oxygen form a covalent bond, the oxygen shares the hydrogen's electron, meaning that the hydrogen has partially lost its electron to the oxygen.

What about the reaction between sodium and chlorine?

$$2\ Na + Cl_2 \rightarrow 2\ NaCl$$

No oxygen is present in this reaction, so the traditional definition of oxidation will not help. But, since sodium is a metal, and metals lose electrons to nonmetals during the formation of an ionic bond, the sodium is oxidized in this reaction.

Oxidation reactions do not happen alone, though. All oxidation reactions are accompanied by **reduction reactions**. Traditionally, reduction has meant the loss of oxygen from a compound. For example, if iron(III) oxide reacts with carbon, the iron(III) oxide is reduced to pure iron.

$$2\ Fe_2O_3 + 3\ C \rightarrow 4\ Fe + 3\ CO_2$$

The iron has lost the oxygen it was bonded with, and the carbon gained oxygen—meaning that it was oxidized.

Today, reduction is defined as the complete or partial gain of electrons. In the above example that produces water, the oxygen is reduced because it gains access to the electrons of two hydrogen atoms. In the sodium chloride example, chlorine, the nonmetal, is reduced. The reactant that is reduced in this type of reaction is called an ***oxidizing agent*** because it allows the other reactant to accept electrons and become oxidized. The reactant that is oxidized is called a ***reducing agent***.

Here is another example of a reaction in which electrons are transferred from one reactant to another:

Mg	+	S	→	MgS
(loses electrons)		(gains electrons)		
(oxidized)		(reduced)		
(reducing agent)		(oxidizing agent)		

Magnesium has two valence electrons. Sulfur has six. If the magnesium gives up its two electrons and sulfur takes them, both elements will have eight valence electrons. Since magnesium is losing electrons, it is being oxidized. Sulfur is reduced because it gains electrons. The oxidized magnesium is the reducing agent in this reaction, and the sulfur is the oxidizing agent.

Any time electrons are transferred between reactants in a chemical reaction, the reaction is called an ***oxidation-reduction reaction***. Oxidation-reduction reactions are also called *redox reactions*.

Not all reactions are redox reactions. Only the ones in which electrons are transferred from one reactant to another are classified as redox reactions. Many single-displacement reactions, combination reactions, decomposition reactions, and combustion reactions are redox reactions. Double displacement reactions never involve the transfer of electrons and are not, therefore, redox reactions. Since acid-base reactions are just a special type of double displacement reaction, they cannot be redox reactions, either.

REACTIONS THAT PRODUCE ELECTRICITY

Since redox reactions involve the movement of electrons, and electricity is simply a stream of moving electrons, redox reactions can be used to produce electricity.

THE CHEMISTRY OF AIRBAGS

Most modern cars come equipped with airbags that are designed to save lives in head-on collisions. The airbags are inflated using a chemical reaction. When a car is involved in a crash, a sensor inside the car detects a rapid decrease in speed. The sensor then flips a switch that completes an electrical circuit. This starts a chemical reaction that inflates the airbag.

When the switch completes the electric circuit, a pellet of sodium azide (NaN_3) is ignited. The sodium azide decomposes into sodium metal and nitrogen gas at about 570°F (300°C). The reaction happens at lightning speed, with the nitrogen gas filling the air bag at 150 to 250 miles per hour (240 to 400 kilometers per hour). In only about 40 milliseconds, the bag is totally full.

$$2\ NaN_3 \rightarrow Na + 3\ N_2\ (gas)$$

Sodium metal is highly reactive, however, and potentially explosive. Because of this, there are two other chemicals in the airbag to get rid of the sodium: potassium nitrate (KNO_3) and silicon dioxide (SiO_2). First, the sodium reacts with the potassium nitrate to produce potassium oxide (K_2O), sodium oxide (Na_2O), and some more nitrogen gas:

$$10\ Na + 2\ KNO_3 \rightarrow K_2O + 5\ Na_2O + N_2$$

Oxides of metals in Group 1 of the periodic table, such as potassium and sodium, are also highly reactive, though. It would not be safe to allow these chemicals to remain in the airbag, so the potassium and sodium oxides then react with silicon dioxide (SiO_2). This reaction forms an alkaline silicate powder. Alkaline silicate, a type of glass, will not burn and the resulting powder is harmless.

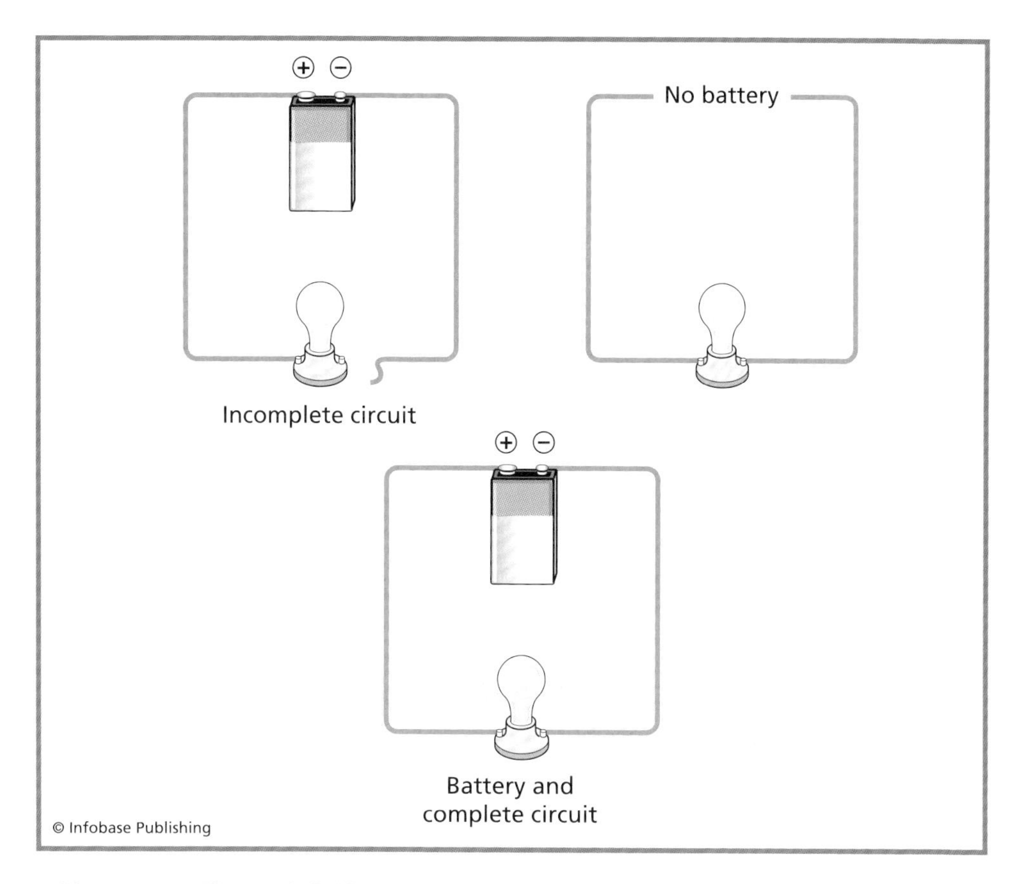

Figure 4.4 The top left illustration is incomplete because the wire is not attached to the lightbulb. The top right illustration is incomplete because the circuit lacks a power source. The bottom illustration is an example of a complete circuit.

Electricity exists not only in homes, schools, and cars, it can be found in nature, too. Lightning, for example, is electricity. Lightning occurs when electrons move from cloud to cloud or from a cloud to the ground. Walking across a carpet and then touching something metallic can produce a nasty little shock, too. The shock happens when electrons jump from a person's finger to the metal that is touched. This is also electricity. Both of these examples involve **static electricity**. Static electricity occurs when two different objects rub together, causing friction. The friction removes some electrons from one of the objects and deposits them on the other object, resulting in a buildup of electrons.

Electricity can also be generated inside a battery. A battery uses a chemical reaction to produce electricity. Inside a battery, there are two different metals in a chemical solution. A redox reaction occurs between the metals and the solution. This solution is called an ***electrolyte*** *solution*. An electrolyte is a substance that can conduct an electric current—the flow of electrons—when it is dissolved in water or melted. All ionic compounds are electrolytes. Most covalent compounds are not.

Because the two metals inside a battery are different, the reaction with the electrolyte frees more electrons from one metal than the other. The two metals are attached at different spots in the battery. These spots are called the *battery's terminals*. The metal that frees more electrons has a positive charge, making it the positive terminal of the battery. The other end of the battery is the negative terminal. If a wire is attached to the positive and negative ends of the battery, the free electrons will flow through the wire. If a lightbulb is attached to that wire, between the battery terminals, the electrons must flow through the lightbulb to get from one terminal to the other. Since the flowing electrons are an electrical current, they are conducting electricity. This electricity will light up the bulb.

Electricity flows in closed loops, or circuits. The circuit must be complete, which means that the loop must be closed, in order for the electrons to flow. In the case of a lightbulb attached to a battery, the electrons will flow from the negative end of the battery, through the wire, and into the lightbulb. Inside the lightbulb is a tiny wire, called a *filament*. When the electrons flow through the filament, it gets very hot and glows. (The gas inside a lightbulb is an inert gas, usually one of the noble gases such as argon or neon.)

A bulb "burns out" when the tiny filament wire breaks. When the filament breaks, it breaks the circuit. The electrons no longer have a closed path to get through to the other wire, so they cannot reach the positive end of the battery, and the bulb will not light. As long as the lightbulb's filament is not broken, a closed loop is made between the negative battery terminal and the positive battery terminal. The electricity will continue to flow until one of the wires is removed from the battery or from the lightbulb.

None of the lightbulbs in a house are connected directly to a battery like the one in this example, but the concept is the same. When a light switch is turned on, the switch closes a circuit inside the wall of the house. Electrons can now flow through the house's wires, into the lightbulb, and back out. When the switch is turned off, the loop is broken again, and the light goes out.

Reaction Rates

Not all chemical reactions happen at the same speed. For example, a bicycle rusts slowly, but a piece of wood burns quickly. The speed of a chemical reaction is called its ***reaction rate***. The reaction rate is calculated by measuring how much product is produced or how much reactant is used up within a certain amount of time.

$$\text{Reaction Rate} = \frac{\text{amount reacted or produced}}{\text{time}}$$

The amount reacted or produced is usually measured in grams, **moles** (A mole is equal to the molecular weight of a substance in grams.), or kilograms. The time measurement might be in seconds, minutes, days, or even years.

In order for atoms, ions, or molecules to react, they must have two things: They must come into contact with one another and they must have enough **kinetic energy**. Kinetic energy is the energy an object has because of its motion. To speed up a reaction, the atoms, ions, or molecules must either collide more often, have more energy when they collide, or both. The following sections explain several ways in which the speed of a chemical reaction can change.

TEMPERATURE

Most chemical reactions speed up when the temperature goes up, and slow down if the temperature decreases.

When the temperature goes up, the molecules move around faster and they have more energy. Increasing the kinetic energy of the atoms, ions, or molecules makes the reaction go faster. The faster the particles are moving, the more they collide with each other.

Decreasing the temperature does exactly the opposite. The particles slow down, so not as many collisions happen. Even if the particles do bump into one another, they do not have enough kinetic energy for the reaction to occur. To see this in action, try the following experiment: Fill one glass with tap water, a second glass with hot water, and a third with ice water. Now, drop one antacid tablet into each glass. Which antacid tablet reacts fastest?

CONCENTRATION

Many chemical reactions take place in solutions. A solution's **concentration** is a measure of the strength of the solution—the number of molecules in a certain volume. The more molecules, the more concentrated the solution. A solution can be made more concentrated by adding more solute to the solvent. For example, a stronger brine solution (remember that brine is very salty water) can be made by adding more salt (the solute) to the water (the solvent).

Increasing the concentration of a solution increases the reaction rate because the particles collide with each other more often.

BANISHING THE BROWN

When an apple is cut, its surface is exposed to oxygen in the air. Iron-containing chemicals inside the apple react with the oxygen and turn the apple brown. This is an oxidation reaction. Keeping cut apples cold will slow down the rate of the chemical reaction that makes them turn brown. Adding lemon juice or orange juice to them will also slow down this process. That is because the juice is an antioxidant and the citric acid acts as an inhibitor.

The more the chemicals bump into one another, the more chances there are that the molecules will react with one another.

Gases can be made more concentrated, too. Think of what happens when a balloon is squeezed: The gas particles inside the balloon get closer together. If the reactants of a chemical reaction are gases and the volume goes down, the reaction rate will usually increase because the gas particles are closer together. The closer they are to one another, the more they will bump into each other.

PARTICLE SIZE

For reactions occurring on solids, the amount of exposed solid will affect the rate of the reaction. Solids that are made of smaller particles instead of one big chunk will usually increase the reaction rate. When the particle size is smaller, there is more surface area available to react. More surface area means more chances for collision between molecules.

For example, steel will burn in an oxygen-rich environment. But the thin fibers of steel wool burn much faster than a bar of steel. As another example, try dropping one whole antacid tablet into a glass of water. Break another antacid tablet into four pieces and

EXPLODING FLOUR

Did you know that dust can explode? Any flammable dust—for example, flour, sawdust, or grain dust—can explode under the correct conditions. The first recorded flour explosion occurred in an Italian flourmill in 1785. There were probably earlier explosions, but this is the first one ever recorded. In this case, a lamp in a bakery supposedly ignited the flour dust. Luckily, no one died in the explosion.

Several conditions need to be met before dust will explode. First, the dust must be combustible. A flour explosion will not happen with an ordinary lump of flour. The flour has to be airborne and have enough air around it to produce a dust cloud. Because flour will burn, its dust cloud is explosive. There also has to be enough oxygen for a combustion reaction to occur. Finally, there needs to be something to ignite the fire.

Figure 5.1 A grain explosion caused the damage to this grain mill.

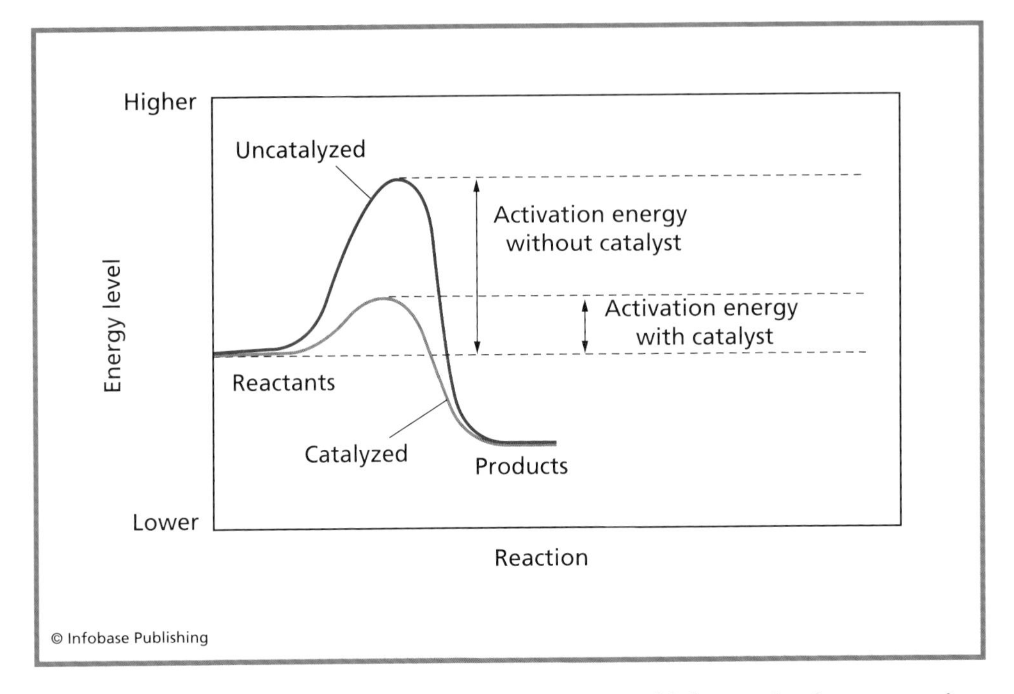

Figure 5.2 The red line in the graph shows that a higher activation energy is needed without the addition of a catalyst. The blue line shows that the activation energy has been lowered by the addition of a catalyst.

drop the pieces into a second glass of water. Finally, crush a third antacid tablet into a powder and put that into a third glass of water. Which antacid tablet reacts fastest?

CATALYSTS AND INHIBITORS

A **catalyst** is a chemical that can speed up a chemical reaction without actually being involved in the reaction itself. During a chemical reaction, a catalyst does not change and is not used up, which means that it can be used over and over again. The **activation energy** is the minimum amount of kinetic energy that colliding particles must have in order for a reaction to happen. Catalysts work by lowering the amount of activation energy needed.

Biological catalysts are called ***enzymes***. All living things use them. For example, normal human body temperature is about 98.6°F (37°C). But many of the chemical reactions needed for the body to function will not happen at this temperature. Enzymes step in to solve the problem. Enzymes will speed up the needed reactions by lowering the activation energy so that the reactions can occur at a lower temperature. As a result, the human body functions just fine at 98.6°F.

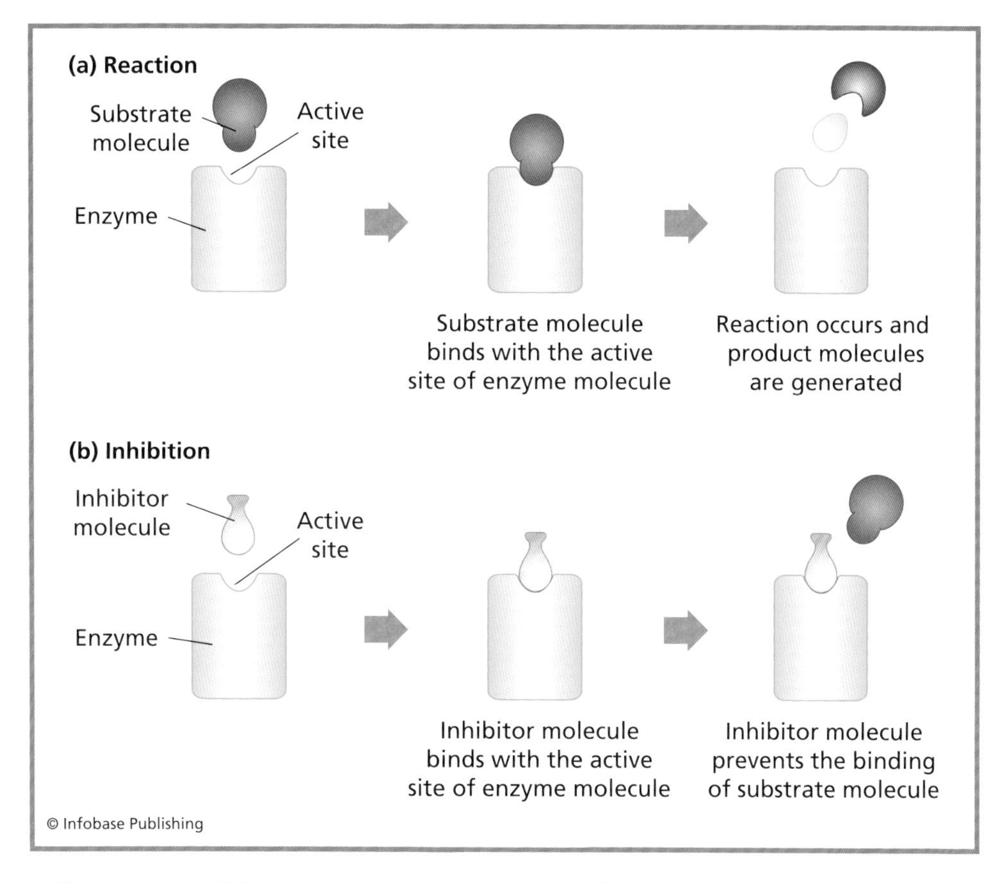

Figure 5.3 (a) The enzyme and substrate molecule fit together like a lock and key to generate a product molecule. (b) An inhibitor molecule can fit with an enzyme and prevent a reaction from occurring.

All enzymes are proteins, and each enzyme catalyzes a specific chemical reaction in the body. The enzyme and the reactants of the chemical reaction fit together like a key in a lock. If the key (the reactant) does not fit the lock (the enzyme) the reaction will not occur.

Inhibitors are substances that interfere with the way a catalyst works. One way inhibitors can interfere with the catalyst is to provide it with the wrong "key." This key fits, just like the reactant fits in the catalyst, but it does not open the "lock." When this happens, the catalyst cannot bind to the correct reactant key. Inhibitors can slow down and, sometimes, even stop chemical reactions.

Reactions in Nature

Life depends on chemical reactions. Chemical reactions take place when plants and animals grow, digest their food, and even when they rest. Some of the chemical reactions that occur in nature take place in the most extreme conditions on the planet, such as near deep-sea vents or in Antarctica. Some reactions are so complex that scientists are not yet sure how they happen.

PHOTOSYNTHESIS

Photosynthesis is the process in which green plants, algae, some types of bacteria, and some protists (one-celled organisms such as slime molds) convert sunlight into food. Any organism that can make its own food from light energy or chemical energy is called an ***autotroph***. Organisms that specifically use light energy to make their own food are called ***photoautotrophs***.

Photosynthesis is an endothermic reaction because energy is required for the reaction to occur. During photosynthesis, energy from the Sun powers a reaction between water and carbon dioxide to produce glucose (a sugar) and oxygen. Sunlight is included in the chemical equation since it provides the energy necessary for the reaction to occur. But because the sunlight is not actually a chemical reactant, it is written above the arrow in the chemical equation.

$$\underset{\text{carbon dioxide}}{6\,CO_2} + \underset{\text{water}}{6\,H_2O} \xrightarrow{\text{sunlight}} \underset{\text{glucose}}{C_6H_{12}O_6} + \underset{\text{oxygen}}{6\,O_2}$$

The glucose produced by this chemical reaction is food for the photoautotroph and, eventually, for the animal that eats the photoautotroph. Glucose is one of the simplest types of **carbohydrate**. All carbohydrates contain the elements carbon, hydrogen, and oxygen. The difference between different carbohydrates comes from the various ways these three elements are arranged in the molecule. Simple carbohydrates, such as glucose, are sugars. Fructose and sucrose are two other simple carbohydrates. Complex carbohydrates are made from several simple carbohydrates that are chemically connected together. Starch and fiber are two kinds of complex carbohydrates.

Carbohydrates provide plants and animals, including humans, with the fuel they need to live; carbohydrates are to living things as gasoline is to a car. Animals, however, cannot make their own carbohydrates like plants do, so animals get the fuel they need by eating the plants that make carbohydrates.

Photosynthesis occurs in specialized parts of a photoautotroph's cells called ***chloroplasts***. A green pigment inside the chloroplast, called ***chlorophyll***, absorbs energy from the Sun to start the reaction. Because photosynthesis is an endothermic reaction, if a photoautotroph is unable to get sunlight—for example, if the photoautotroph is in a dark place—photosynthesis will not occur.

RESPIRATION

The oxygen produced by photoautotrophs during the photosynthetic process is essential for life on Earth because organisms use the oxygen for **respiration**. Respiration is the process living organisms use to get the energy they need to live. Sometimes people refer to respiration as "breathing," but it is not the same thing. Breathing means taking air into the lungs and exhaling carbon dioxide. Respiration, on the other hand, occurs at the cellular level and provides living things with the energy they need. Like photosynthesis, respiration also occurs in specialized parts of cells. The specialized parts of cells that carry out respiration are called the ***mitochondria***.

The respiration reaction is, basically, the opposite of the photosynthesis reaction. During respiration, glucose within the cells reacts with oxygen to produce carbon dioxide, water, and energy.

$$\underset{\text{glucose}}{C_6H_{12}O_6} + \underset{\text{oxygen}}{6\,O_2} \rightarrow \underset{\text{carbon dioxide}}{6\,CO_2} + \underset{\text{water}}{6\,H_2O} + \text{energy}$$

The respiration reaction produces the energy that living things need in order to grow. Since respiration gives off energy, it is an exothermic reaction. Plants use the glucose they make during photosynthesis when they respire. Animals get the glucose they need by eating plants or other animals.

DIGESTION

Animals need to digest food in order to produce the glucose their cells need to respire. **Digestion** is a multistep process during which food is broken down into substances that can be absorbed by the body. Enzymes speed up digestion by catalyzing the breakdown of food.

Digestion starts in the mouth, where saliva breaks down starch (a complex carbohydrate) into sugar (a simple one). This is why chewing on a piece of bread for a long time makes it start to taste

CAVE FORMATION

When water falls through the atmosphere as rain, ice, or snow, the water can combine with carbon dioxide in the air and produce carbonic acid.

CO_2	+	H_2O	→	H_2CO_3
carbon dioxide		water		carbonic acid

Once on the ground, the water moves through the soil and picks up more carbon dioxide from decaying plants and animals, forming more carbonic acid. As carbonic acid passes through the soil and reaches the rock below, it can seep into the cracks and pores of rocks. When carbonic acid encounters one type of rock—limestone—the acid dissolves the rock. In areas where much of the underlying rock is limestone, certain landforms such as caves, sinkholes, and potholes, are common.

Limestone is mostly made up of the mineral calcite, or calcium carbonate ($CaCO_3$). As the calcium carbonate rock dissolves in the slightly acidic water, spaces and even caves develop underground. If carbonic acid dissolves all the way through the rock and into a cave below the Earth's surface, the resulting solution contains calcium hydrogen carbonate (calcium bicarbonate).

$CaCO_3$ (s)	+	H_2CO_3 (aq)	→	$Ca(HCO_3)_2$ (aq)
calcium carbonate or limestone		carbonic acid or $H_2O + CO_2$		calcium hydrogen carbonate or calcium bicarbonate

As the calcium bicarbonate solution drips through cracks in the rock and into an underground cavern, some carbon dioxide bubbles out of the solution.

$Ca(HCO_3)_2$ (aq)	→	$CaCO_3$ (s)	+	H_2O (l)	+	CO_2 (g)
calcium bicarbonate		calcium carbonate		water		carbon dioxide gas

Without the carbon dioxide, the water can no longer hold the calcium carbonate in the solution, either. As a result, calcium carbonate precipitates out of the solution as solid limestone. During the course of tens of thousands of years, the precipitating calcium carbonate produces formations inside the caves, called *speleothems*. The most common speleothems are **stalactites** and **stalagmites**.

Stalactites hang from the ceiling of limestone caves. They look like icicles and occur at cracks where water flows through the limestone and into the cave. Sometimes water containing some dissolved calcium carbonate will drip off the tip of a stalactite and onto the floor of the cave. In these places, stalagmites will form on the cave floor. Sometimes a stalactite and a stalagmite will connect and make a column.

When the ceiling of a cave collapses, it forms a sinkhole. In the United States, sinkholes are most often found in Florida, Texas, Alabama, Missouri, Kentucky, Tennessee, and Pennsylvania. That is because these states have a lot of limestone rock.

Figure 6.1 An example of stalagmites and stalactites in a limestone cave.

sweet. It tastes sweet because saliva contains an enzyme called *amylase* that chemically changes the starch in the bread into sugar. Digestion continues in the stomach, where the high acid content inhibits the enzymes needed to further break down carbohydrates. The high acid content of the stomach does help break down proteins, but at this point in the digestion process, carbohydrate digestion basically stops.

Once the proteins have been broken down and the food has moved past the stomach and into the upper part of the small intestines, an organ called the pancreas produces bicarbonate ions (HCO_3^-) to neutralize the stomach acid. This reaction occurs in the duodenum, where the small intestines joins the stomach.

The enzyme amylase is present in the small intestines, too, so the digestion of carbohydrates can continue there. The carbohydrates eventually are broken down into their simplest form—glucose—which cells can use during respiration to produce the energy the body needs to function.

CHEMOSYNTHESIS

Some bacteria living deep in the ocean can also make their own food. Since sunlight cannot reach the deepest parts of the ocean, these bacteria make their food using a process called ***chemosynthesis***. Instead of using sunlight, these organisms make their food using chemical compounds.

The chemicals come from cracks on the ocean floor called ***hydrothermal vents***. Hydrothermal vents are most often found where the sea floor is spreading due to the movement of sections of Earth's crust. Seawater enters the cracks produced by the spreading plates and is heated by hot magma lying under the surface. The water can reach temperatures as high as 750°F (400°C).

Sometimes, the vents have what scientists call *chimneys* on them. These chimneys are formed when the super hot, chemical-filled water hits the almost freezing seawater and some of the dissolved chemicals precipitate out of solution. Some vent chimneys can grow as tall as 30 feet (about 9 meters) in just 18 months. One such chimney in the Pacific Ocean, called "Godzilla," grew to the height of a 15-story building before it fell over.

Most of the deep, deep ocean has little life in it because it is too cold, only a few degrees above freezing, and, with no sunlight, there is no food to support life. But the area around these deep-sea vents

LACTOSE INTOLERANCE

When a person cannot digest lactose, the main sugar in milk, that person has a condition called *lactose intolerance*. People with lactose intolerance cannot digest lactose because their bodies do not make enough of the enzyme lactase. Cells in the small intestines normally produce lactase. In people with normal amounts of lactase, food and drink products that contain lactose get broken down in the small intestines. But in a person with lactose intolerance, the lactose moves through the small intestine without being broken down. Once the lactose enters the large intestines, the bacteria that live inside the large intestine break down the lactose to make energy for themselves. As the bacteria break down the milk sugar, they produce alcohol in a process called *fermentation*.

Unfortunately for people with lactose intolerance, another product of fermentation is carbon dioxide gas. A build-up of this gas in the large intestine can cause some uncomfortable symptoms including nausea, cramps, bloating, gas, and diarrhea. For a lactose intolerant person, symptoms usually appear 30 minutes to a couple of hours after eating or drinking dairy products. There is no "cure" for lactose intolerance, but it can be managed either by avoiding products that contain lactose or by taking medication that contains lactase.

Figure 6.2 Hydrothermal vents are cracks in the Earth's surface generally found within deep ocean waters. Hot magma enters the cracks and heats the icy water, allowing bacteria to grow and feed a vast array of marine life.

is an exception. These areas are teeming with life because the water is warmer there and plentiful bacteria can provide food. The bacteria make their own food by oxidizing sulfide compounds—such as hydrogen sulfide (H_2S)—that come out of the vents. The bacteria then become food for more than 300 species of animals, including tubeworms, fish, crabs, shrimp, and clams. All of these animals depend on the bacteria for food in one way or another. Some of the animals living near the vents just eat the bacteria. Others eat the animals that eat the bacteria.

Around deep-sea vents lives a very interesting species of animal: the tubeworm. Some tubeworms can grow to be almost 8 feet (3 m) long. They were first discovered in the 1970s around some hydrothermal vents near the Galapagos Islands off the coast of South America. Since then many tubeworms have been found at deep-sea vents all over the world.

Tubeworms that live around hydrothermal vents do not have a mouth, eyes, or a stomach. In order to get food, a tubeworm invites bacteria into its body to live and make food there. Scientists have found that tubeworms are born with both a mouth and a digestive tract, which is how the bacteria enter the worm. But as a worm grows, its digestive tract disappears, making it completely reliant on the bacteria that enter its mouth when it is young. This relationship works out well for the bacteria, too, because they get a nice, safe place to live. This kind of relationship—one in which both parties cooperate and benefit—is called a ***symbiotic relationship***.

BIOLUMINESCENCE

Animals do not just use chemical reactions to produce food. Like the fireflies, they sometimes use chemical reactions to produce light. The ability to produce light through a chemical reaction is called *bioluminescence*.

With the exception of fireflies, a bioluminescent fungus called *foxfire*, and some types of worms and insects, bioluminescence is fairly limited among land animals. But almost 90% of the animals living in the deep ocean, where sunlight cannot penetrate, are bioluminescent. (The "deep ocean" is defined as starting at about 650 to 3,000 feet (about 200 to 1,000 m) deep.) The glow produced by bioluminescent land-dwelling animals comes in many colors. But most sea animals produce light that appears blue-green.

Bioluminescence is the result of a very efficient chemical reaction. Nearly all the energy produced by the reaction is turned into light, and almost no heat is given off. Compare that to a lightbulb in which only 3% of the energy is turned into light, while the other 97% is wasted as heat. That is why it is not a good idea to touch a lightbulb that has been on for a while—it's hot!

Three chemicals must be present in order for bioluminescence to occur: oxygen, luciferin, and the enzyme luciferase. The type of luciferin present is different in different animals. Because enzymes are specific to the chemicals they bind with, the luciferase is also

HOW DO POLAR BEARS STAY WARM?

Fat comes in two colors: white and brown. The body can use white fat as an energy source. White fat is also useful for keeping an organism warm because of its insulating properties; it also cushions the body. Most of the fat in the body is white fat.

Brown fat, however, can actually produce heat. This heat production is called *thermogenesis*. Brown fat cells contain a lot of mitochondria, also known as a cell's "power plant" because they are the primary source of energy in cells. The energy is produced during respiration. The presence of so many mitochondria within brown fat cells is the key to tissue's ability to produce heat.

The presence of so many mitochondria is also what makes the fat appear brown. Brown fat makes up about 5% of the body weight of human newborns, preventing the baby from getting too cold. As humans grow, this tissue gradually loses its mitochondria and becomes more like white fat, although some humans keep their brown fat into adulthood. Brown fat deposits are also found in many hibernating mammals, such as polar bears, helping them keep warm through the long winters.

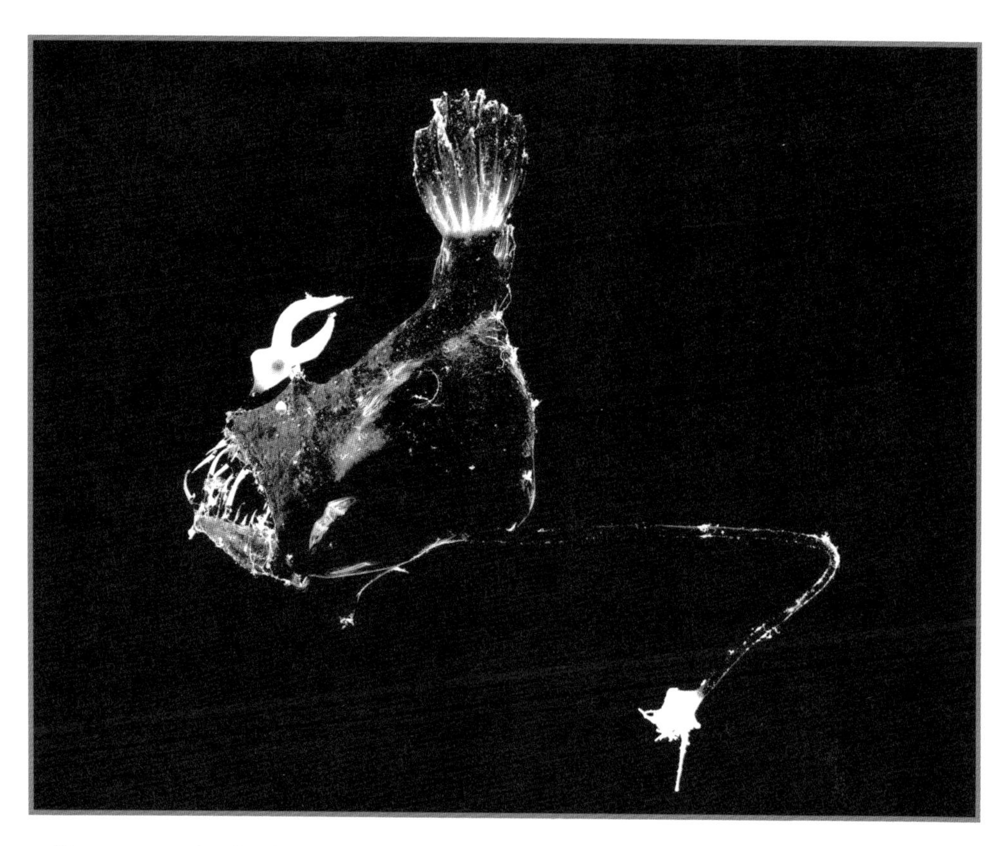

Figure 6.3 In the dark ocean, an anglerfish would be hard to see if it wasn't bioluminescent. The fish's unusual forehead appendage, like a fishing lure, attracts unsuspecting prey to its mouth.

unique to the particular animal. The luciferase must match the particular type of luciferin made by that animal, or else bioluminescence will not occur.

Animals use bioluminescence for several different reasons. The bioluminescent squid, for example, uses bioluminescence to get away from predators. The squid squirts out a big cloud of glowing chemicals and escapes from danger while the predator is distracted. Tiny, shrimp-like animals called *krill* also use their light power to try to avoid being eaten. For krill, there is safety in numbers, so millions of these tiny creatures clump together and use their bioluminescence to communicate with one another. This helps them stay together and confuse their predators with a huge glowing, swirling mass.

Like fireflies, Bermuda fireworms use their colorful bioluminescent show to try to attract a mate. Anglerfish are trying to attract something, too—but instead of a mate, they are trying to attract food. The anglerfish lives very deep in the ocean, below 3,000 feet (1,000 m). These fish have a glowing light dangling like a fishing lure from their foreheads. They use this to trick small fish and shrimp into swimming near their mouths, where the anglerfish can catch them easily.

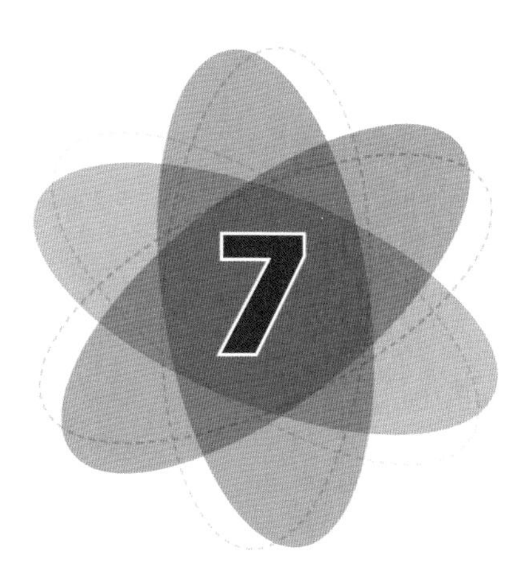

Amazing Reactions

Amazing chemical reactions do not only happen in living things. The Statue of Liberty is green because of a chemical reaction. Light sticks used on Halloween work because of a chemical reaction. In fact, chefs, doctors, and police officers all use chemical reactions to help them do their jobs.

THE STATUE OF LIBERTY

The Statue of Liberty is made of about 31 tons (about 46 metric tons) of copper. But copper is shiny and, well, copper-colored—certainly not green. The Statue of Liberty is green because when copper is exposed to oxygen, it is oxidized. Copper oxide is green and dull, rather than reddish-orange and shiny.

When a metal develops a coating of oxidized metal like the Statue of Liberty has, the film is called a ***patina***. A patina is a thin surface layer of corrosion, but only the outer layer has oxidized.

Figure 7.1 Statues, buildings, and other relics made of certain elements can undergo physical changes because of chemical reactions. a) This prototype face of the Statue of Liberty is made of copper, a bright, red-orange metal. b) The actual Statue of Liberty is made of copper, but because of exposure to elements in the air, the copper has been oxidized to create a thin, pale green layer called a *patina*.

Because of this outer skin of copper oxide, the rest of the Statue of Liberty is protected from further corrosion. This is why no one cleans the patina off the Statue of Liberty. If they did, she would corrode away.

LIGHT STICKS

Light sticks, or glow sticks, are plastic tubes that contain glass vials of chemicals. When the plastic stick is bent, the glass vial breaks. This allows the chemicals inside the glass vial to come into contact with the chemicals inside the plastic part of the light stick. This starts a chemical reaction that gives off light. Light that is produced by a chemical reaction and does not produce heat is called ***chemiluminescence***. Each light stick also contains a fluorescent dye, which is what produces the light stick's color. Different dyes produce different colors.

During the chemical reaction that occurs inside a light stick, some electrons are boosted to higher energy levels. The electrons will then fall back to their normal energy levels, closer to their nuclei. When the electrons return to their normal energy levels, they release energy in the form of **photons**, or light.

Depending on which chemicals are used inside the light stick, the reaction can last for a just a couple of minutes or possibly up to several hours. The reaction can be sped up by heating up the light stick. It will give off a brighter light, but for a shorter period of time. Putting the light stick in the freezer can slow down the chemical reaction, but it will not stop it. The light will be much dimmer and the reaction will last longer.

BAKING

Many chemical reactions occur in the kitchen. For example, some types of breads, called *yeast breads*, rely on the chemical reactions of tiny **microbes** to make them look and taste the way they do. The microbes, in this case, are yeast spores mixed into the bread dough. Yeast spores are tiny living things that can only be seen under a microscope. When yeast is mixed into bread dough, they feed on the carbohydrates in the flour and produce carbon dioxide gas and alcohol. This process is called ***fermentation***.

The carbon dioxide gas that is produced during fermentation is what makes yeast bread rise. When the bread is cooked, the heat gets rid of the carbon dioxide and alcohol that the yeast produced, leaving behind tiny holes where the carbon dioxide bubbles burst. These holes make the bread light and fluffy.

Other types of bread, called *quick breads*, do not use yeast. These breads instead rely on the reaction between baking soda and an acid to rise. If baking soda is mixed with an acid, it makes carbon dioxide, too. Sour milk or buttermilk both contain lactic acid and are often used to make this reaction happen.

The reaction between baking soda and an acid can easily be seen. Put a teaspoon of baking soda in a dish, add a teaspoon of vinegar, and watch it bubble. The baking soda is a base. The vinegar is an acid. The bubbling comes from the carbon dioxide gas created by the reaction. The solution that is left over is neutral.

BLAST OFF!

It takes a lot of force to get a space shuttle out of the grip of Earth's gravity. Two solid rocket boosters filled with a solid mixture of ammonium perchlorate and aluminum metal, called the propellant, produce most of that force. The rockets also contain a catalyst made of iron oxide, which speeds up the burning of the propellant. Another material called the *binder* holds everything together. All together, the propellant, the catalyst, and the binder make up the solid material inside the rocket boosters.

Once the propellant starts burning, it cannot be stopped. The reaction looks like this:

$$10\,Al + 6\,NH_4ClO_4 \rightarrow 4\,Al_2O_3 + 2\,AlCl_3 + 12\,H_2O + 3\,N_2$$

aluminum	ammonium perchlorate	aluminum oxide	aluminum chloride	water vapor	nitrogen gas

The oxygen from the ammonium perchlorate reacts with the aluminum metal to produce aluminum oxide. The other products are aluminum chloride, water vapor, and nitrogen gas.

This reaction is extremely exothermic and heats the inside of the solid rocket booster to about 5,800°F (3,200°C). This extremely high temperature causes the two gases, nitrogen and water vapor, to expand rapidly. This is

MEDICAL SCIENCE

Doctors use their knowledge of chemical reactions every day to help people lead healthier lives. For example, a doctor might measure the amount of enzymes being produced by the liver to see if that organ is functioning normally.

A doctor might also use a chemical reaction to test a patient's blood glucose (sugar) level. Remember that during digestion, carbohydrates are broken down into the simplest sugar, glucose.

what provides the upward thrust needed to get the space shuttle into space.

The reaction happens quickly: All the fuel in the solid rocket boosters is used up in about two minutes. When all of the propellant is used up, the boosters separate from the shuttle and fall back to Earth and into the Atlantic Ocean, where a ship picks them up and tows them back to Florida so they can be reused. About 71% of the upward thrust needed to get the shuttle into orbit comes from the solid rocket boosters.

While the solid rocket boosters are doing their jobs, the shuttle's engines are also running. These engines use fuel stored in an external fuel tank attached to the shuttle to provide the rest of the thrust required to get the shuttle out of Earth's gravitational grip. The tank actually contains two separate fuel tanks. One contains liquid hydrogen and the other has liquid oxygen. When these two chemicals react with one another, water vapor is formed. The reaction also produces extremely high temperatures—around 6,000°F (3,300°C). The water vapor produces the extra lift the shuttle needs to get out of Earth's orbit. Like the solid rocket boosters, the external tank separates from the shuttle when the fuel is gone. Unlike the boosters, by the time the external tank is released from the shuttle, it is outside of Earth's atmosphere and it burns up as it reenters the atmosphere.

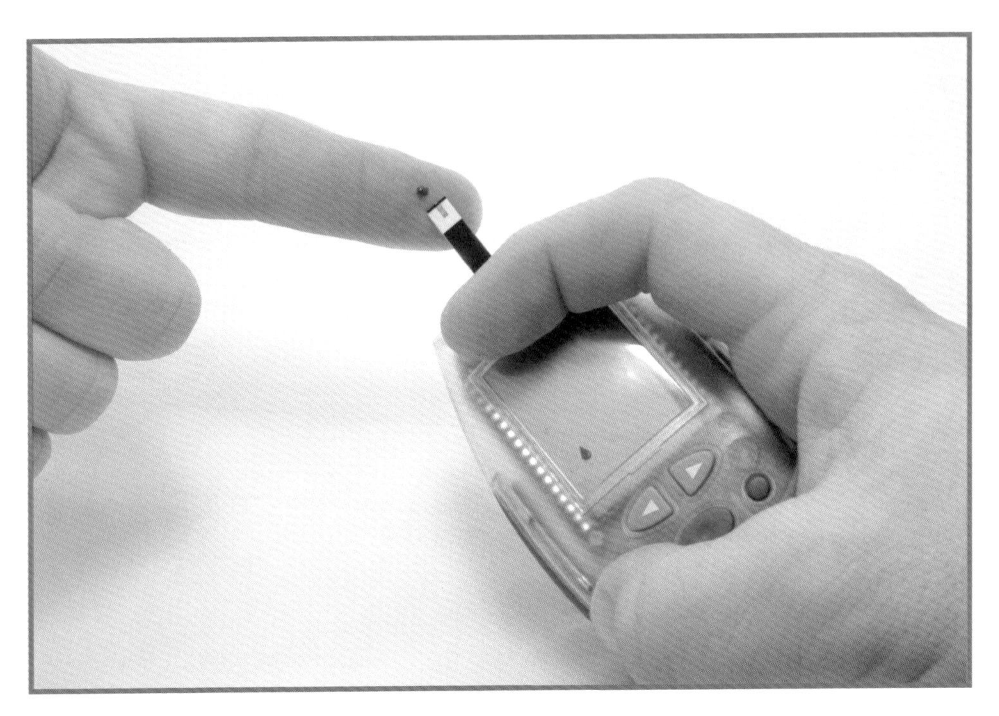

Figure 7.2 By understanding the chemical reactions of the body, doctors are able to diagnose diseases, such as diabetes. Diabetic patients must use a special tool to check their blood sugar levels several times a day.

Cells in the body need glucose in order to produce the energy that the body needs. Insulin is a hormone produced by the pancreas in response to high blood glucose levels. Insulin attaches to the body's cells and allows the cells to absorb sugar from the blood. Without insulin, the cells cannot get the sugar they need to carry out cellular respiration. The pancreas of a person born with Type I diabetes does not make insulin. People with Type I diabetes must take **synthetic**, or human-made, insulin. They can get extremely sick without their insulin shots. Because a diabetic person's cells cannot absorb glucose from the bloodstream, high blood glucose levels can help a doctor diagnose someone with diabetes. A person with diabetes must test his blood glucose level several times per day. If his blood sugar is too high, he must either take insulin or some other drug to lower his blood sugar levels.

Doctors and medical laboratory technicians rely on the chemical reactions between a person's blood and chemicals added to their blood sample to detect, diagnose, and treat diseases. Medical lab technicians, for example, use a chemical reaction to match blood types for blood transfusions. They also use chemical reactions to test for drug levels in the blood to show how a patient is responding to treatment.

Antibiotic drugs also use chemical reactions to kill bacteria. Some antibiotics work by stopping the chemical reactions bacteria need to live or reproduce. Others rely on chemical reactions to prevent bacteria from building strong cell walls.

FORENSIC SCIENCE

Chemical reactions can help the police solve crimes, too. Luminol, for example, is a chemical that reacts with blood. Police use luminol to look for traces of blood at crime scenes. When luminol comes into contact with hemoglobin, a chemical found in blood, it produces light. In the chemical reaction between luminol and hemoglobin, the reactants have more energy than the products of the reaction, so the reaction gives off energy in the form of visible light photons. This reaction is chemiluminescent.

The police also use breathalyzers to see if someone has been drinking and driving. Some types of breathalyzers contain a red-orange chemical that turns green if there is alcohol present in the air a person exhales. Others use crystals that turn from yellow to blue. If all of the crystals change color, the person's blood alcohol level is over 0.1%, the legal limit in most states. Other types of breath alcohol testing equipment measure the electric current generated by the chemical reaction that changes ethyl alcohol, the type of alcohol in alcoholic drinks, into acetic acid. The higher the person's blood alcohol level, the higher the electrical current.

POLYMERS

Polymers are long, repeating chemical chains made up of smaller molecules called *monomers*. DNA is an example of a biological polymer. It is made up of monomers called *nucleotides*. The backbone of DNA is made up of a repeating sugar-phosphate monomer string. There are four different kinds of nucleotides in DNA: adenine, guanine, cytosine, and thymine. The only difference between the four is that each one contains a different nitrogen-containing chemical called a *base*.

South American Indians discovered another natural polymer. They found that if they cut the bark of some rainforest trees, a milky-white liquid came out. This liquid is now called *latex*. When Europeans arrived in the New World, they found that if they rubbed the latex over pencil marks, the pencil marks rubbed off. They called this material "rubber." Some British explorers took rubber tree seeds back to England and grew the trees there. Today, 90% of the world's rubber comes from the descendants of those seeds.

Amber, or fossilized tree sap, is also made up of polymers. Pine trees contain a polymer called *rosin*. Violinists use rosin to make their bows slide more easily over the violin's strings. Gymnasts also use rosin to improve their grips on uneven bars and other gymnastics equipment. Rosin is used in some kinds of soap, too.

Insects also produce polymers. For example, silk is made by a caterpillar called a *silkworm*. One silkworm's cocoon can contain as much as 900 to 3,000 feet (300 to 900 m) of silk thread. An insect called the *Laccifer lacca*—or just Lac, for short—lives on trees in India and Southeast Asia. The insects drink the sap from the trees they are living on and produce a polymer that is used to make lacquer and shellac. People use these varnishes to coat and protect ships, houses, wood floors, furniture, and other objects made of wood.

All of these polymers are found in nature. There are many synthetic polymers, too. For example, acrylics used in paint, winter coats, and bed comforters are polymers. Polyethylene is the plastic

THE ACCIDENTAL DISCOVERY OF TEFLON

Roy Plunkett did not set out to invent Teflon. He discovered this polymer by accident while working in a lab in 1938. Plunkett was trying to make a new chlorofluorocarbon (CFC)—a chemical compound that contains chlorine, fluorine, and carbon and used to be a common ingredient in aerosol spray propellants, degreasing agents, foam packing material, and refrigerants.

In order to make the new CFC, Plunkett made 100 pounds (45 kilograms) of tetrafluoroethylene (TFE) gas. It contains only carbon and fluorine. Plunkett planned to add chlorine to the gas later, so he stored the containers of TFE gas at a very low temperature—about –109.3°F (–78.5°C)—until he was ready for them.

But when Plunkett and an assistant tried to remove the TFE gas from the container, nothing came out. Stumped, Plunkett weighed the container and found out that it still weighed the same as when he put it in storage. That meant that there was something in the container, but why wasn't the TFE gas coming out?

Plunkett and his assistant decided to cut open the containers. When they did, they found a white, waxy powder inside. Plunkett tested the powder. He found that it was chemically inert and heat resistant. He also found out that it had a very low surface friction. Because of this low surface friction, most things would not stick to the powder. The TFE gas in the container had polymerized to produce this new substance. The new substance's chemical name is polytetrafluoroethylene (PTFE). It was later named *Teflon*. Teflon is used to protect fabrics and in bakeware to prevent food from sticking to pots and pans.

used to make beverage bottles, and polystyrene is used to make coffee cups and the foam-like "peanuts" used to cushion breakable items in shipping boxes. Many things used in everyday life are made up of natural or synthetic polymers.

LIFE DEPENDS ON CHEMICAL REACTIONS

Whether chemical reactions are used to make plastics, diagnose disease, catch criminals, or for entertainment purposes, life would be very different without them. Indeed, without certain chemical reactions, life would not exist at all. When we eat, light a candle, watch a firefly or fireworks light up the summer sky, or engage in any number of other activities, chemical reactions occur. In fact, they are happening all around us—all the time.

PERIODIC TABLE OF THE ELEMENTS

Key: 3 (Atomic number) — Li (Symbol) — 6.941 (Atomic mass)

1 IA	2 IIA		3 IIIB	4 IVB	5 VB	6 VIB	7 VIIB	8 VIIIB	9 VIIIB
1 H 1.00794									
3 Li 6.941	4 Be 9.0122								
11 Na 22.9898	12 Mg 24.3051								
19 K 39.0938	20 Ca 40.078		21 Sc 44.9559	22 Ti 47.867	23 V 50.9415	24 Cr 51.9962	25 Mn 54.938	26 Fe 55.845	27 Co 58.9332
37 Rb 85.4678	38 Sr 87.62		39 Y 88.906	40 Zr 91.224	41 Nb 92.9064	42 Mo 95.94	43 Tc (98)	44 Ru 101.07	45 Rh 102.9055
55 Cs 132.9054	56 Ba 137.328	57-70 ☆	71 Lu 174.967	72 Hf 178.49	73 Ta 180.948	74 W 183.84	75 Re 186.207	76 Os 190.23	77 Ir 192.217
87 Fr (223)	88 Ra (226)	89-102 ★	103 Lr (260)	104 Rf (261)	105 Db (262)	106 Sg (266)	107 Bh (262)	108 Hs (263)	109 Mt (268)

☆ Lanthanides	57 La 138.9055	58 Ce 140.115	59 Pr 140.908	60 Nd 144.24	61 Pm (145)
★ Actinides	89 Ac (227)	90 Th 232.0381	91 Pa 231.036	92 U 238.0289	93 Np (237)

Numbers in parentheses are atomic mass numbers of most stable isotopes.

Key	
(white box)	Metals
(white box)	Non-metals
(shaded box)	Metalloids

10 VIIIB	11 IB	12 IIB	13 IIIA	14 IVA	15 VA	16 VIA	17 VIIA	18 VIIIA
								2 He 4.0026
			5 B 10.81	6 C 12.011	7 N 14.0067	8 O 15.9994	9 F 18.9984	10 Ne 20.1798
			13 Al 26.9815	14 Si 28.0855	15 P 30.9738	16 S 32.067	17 Cl 35.4528	18 Ar 39.948
28 Ni 58.6934	29 Cu 63.546	30 Zn 65.409	31 Ga 69.723	32 Ge 72.61	33 As 74.9216	34 Se 78.96	35 Br 79.904	36 Kr 83.798
46 Pd 106.42	47 Ag 107.8682	48 Cd 112.412	49 In 114.818	50 Sn 118.711	51 Sb 121.760	52 Te 127.60	53 I 126.9045	54 Xe 131.29
78 Pt 195.08	79 Au 196.9655	80 Hg 200.59	81 Tl 204.3833	82 Pb 207.2	83 Bi 208.9804	84 Po (209)	85 At (210)	86 Rn (222)
110 Ds (271)	111 Rg (272)	112 Uub (277)						

62 Sm 150.36	63 Eu 151.966	64 Gd 157.25	65 Tb 158.9253	66 Dy 162.500	67 Ho 164.9303	68 Er 167.26	69 Tm 168.9342	70 Yb 173.04
94 Pu (244)	95 Am 243	96 Cm (247)	97 Bk (247)	98 Cf (251)	99 Es (252)	100 Fm (257)	101 Md (258)	102 No (259)

ELECTRON CONFIGURATIONS

3 Li $[He]\ 2s^1$	
3	Atomic number
Li	Symbol
$[He]\ 2s^1$	Electron configuration

1 IA ns^1	2 ns^2		3 IIIB	4 IVB	5 VB	6 VIB	7 VIIB	8 VIIIB	9 VIIIB
1 H $1s^1$									
3 Li $[He]2s^1$	4 Be $[He]2s^2$								
11 Na $[Ne]3s^1$	12 Mg $[Ne]3s^2$								
19 K $[Ar]4s^1$	20 Ca $[Ar]\ 4s^2$		21 Sc $[Ar]4s^2 3d^1$	22 Ti $[Ar]4s^2 3d^2$	23 V $[Ar]4s^2 3d^3$	24 Cr $[Ar]4s^1 3d^5$	25 Mn $[Ar]4s^2 3d^5$	26 Fe $[Ar]4s^2 3d^6$	27 Co $[Ar]4s^2 3d^7$
37 Rb $[Kr]5s^1$	38 Sr $[Kr]5s^2$		39 Y $[Kr]5s^2 4d^1$	40 Zr $[Kr]5s^2 4d^2$	41 Nb $[Kr]5s^1 4d^4$	42 Mo $[Kr]5s^1 4d^5$	43 Tc $[Kr]5s^1 4d^6$	44 Ru $[Kr]5s^1 4d^7$	45 Rh $[Kr]5s^1 4d^8$
55 Cs $[Xe]6s^1$	56 Ba $[Xe]6s^2$	57-70 ☆	71 Lu $[Xe]$ $6s^2 4f^{14} 5d^1$	72 Hf $[Xe]$ $4f^{14} 6s^2 5d^2$	73 Ta $[Xe]6s^2 5d^3$	74 W $[Xe]6s^2 5d^4$	75 Re $[Xe]6s^2 5d^5$	76 Os $[Xe]6s^2 5d^6$	77 Ir $[Xe]6s^2 5d^7$
87 Fr $[Rn]7s^1$	88 Ra $[Rn]7s^2$	89-102 ★	103 Lr $[Rn]$ $7s^2 5f^{14} 6d^1$	104 Rf $[Rn]7s^2 6d^2$	105 Db $[Rn]7s^2 6d^3$	106 Sg $[Rn]7s^2 6d^4$	107 Bh $[Rn]7s^2 6d^5$	108 Hs $[Rn]7s^2 6d^6$	109 Mt $[Rn]7s^2 6d^7$

☆ Lanthanides	57 La $[Xe]$ $6s^2 5d^1$	58 Ce $[Xe]$ $6s^2 4f^1 5d^1$	59 Pr $[Xe]$ $6s^2 4f^3 5d^0$	60 Nd $[Xe]$ $6s^2 4f^4 5d^0$	61 Pm $[Xe]$ $6s^2 4f^5 5d^0$
★ Actinides	89 Ac $[Rn]7s^2 6d^1$	90 Th $[Rn]$ $7s^2 5f^0 6d^2$	91 Pa $[Rn]$ $7s^2 5f^2 6d^1$	92 U $[Rn]$ $7s^2 5f^3 6d^1$	93 Np $[Rn]$ $7s^2 5f^4 6d^1$

10 VIIIB	11 IB	12 IIB	13 IIIA ns^2np^1	14 IVA ns^2np^2	15 VA ns^2np^3	16 VIA ns^2np^4	17 VIIA ns^2np^5	18 VIIIA ns^2np^6
								2 He $1s^2$
			5 B $[He]2s^22p^1$	6 C $[He]2s^22p^2$	7 N $[He]2s^22p^3$	8 O $[He]2s^22p^4$	9 F $[He]2s^22p^5$	10 Ne $[He]2s^22p^6$
			13 Al $[Ne]3s^23p^1$	14 Si $[Ne]3s^23p^2$	15 P $[Ne]3s^23p^3$	16 S $[Ne]3s^23p^4$	17 Cl $[Ne]3s^23p^5$	18 Ar $[Ne]3s^23p^6$
28 Ni $[Ar]4s^23d^8$	29 Cu $[Ar]4s^13d^{10}$	30 Zn $[Ar]4s^23d^{10}$	31 Ga $[Ar]4s^24p^1$	32 Ge $[Ar]4s^24p^2$	33 As $[Ar]4s^24p^3$	34 Se $[Ar]4s^24p^4$	35 Br $[Ar]4s^24p^5$	36 Kr $[Ar]4s^24p^6$
46 Pd $[Kr]4d^{10}$	47 Ag $[Kr]5s^14d^{10}$	48 Cd $[Kr]5s^24d^{10}$	49 In $[Kr]5s^25p^1$	50 Sn $[Kr]5s^25p^2$	51 Sb $[Kr]5s^25p^3$	52 Te $[Kr]5s^25p^4$	53 I $[Kr]5s^25p^5$	54 Xe $[Kr]5s^25p^6$
78 Pt $[Xe]6s^15d^9$	79 Au $[Xe]6s^15d^{10}$	80 Hg $[Xe]6s^25d^{10}$	81 Tl $[Xe]6s^26p^1$	82 Pb $[Xe]6s^26p^2$	83 Bi $[Xe]6s^26p^3$	84 Po $[Xe]6s^26p^4$	85 At $[Xe]6s^26p^5$	86 Rn $[Xe]6s^26p^6$
110 Ds $[Rn]7s^16d^9$	111 Rg $[Rn]7s^16d^{10}$	112 Uub $[Rn]7s^26d^{10}$						

62 Sm	63 Eu	64 Gd	65 Tb	66 Dy	67 Ho	68 Er	69 Tm	70 Yb
[Xe] $6s^24f^65d^0$	[Xe] $6s^24f^75d^0$	[Xe] $6s^24f^75d^1$	[Xe] $6s^24f^95d^0$	[Xe] $6s^24f^{10}5d^0$	[Xe] $6s^24f^{11}5d^0$	[Xe] $6s^24f^{12}5d^0$	[Xe] $6s^24f^{13}5d^0$	[Xe] $6s^24f^{14}5d^0$
94 Pu	95 Am	96 Cm	97 Bk	98 Cf	99 Es	100 Fm	101 Md	102 No
[Rn] $7s^25f^66d^0$	[Rn] $7s^25f^76d^0$	[Rn] $7s^25f^76d^1$	[Rn] $7s^25f^96d^0$	[Rn] $7s^25f^{10}6d^0$	[Rn] $7s^25f^{11}6d^0$	[Rn] $7s^25f^{12}6d^0$	[Rn] $7s^25f^{13}6d^0$	[Rn] $7s^25f^{14}6d^1$

TABLE OF ATOMIC MASSES

ELEMENT	SYMBOL	ATOMIC NUMBER	ATOMIC MASS
Actinium	Ac	89	(227)
Aluminum	Al	13	26.9815
Americium	Am	95	243
Antimony	Sb	51	121.76
Argon	Ar	18	39.948
Arsenic	As	33	74.9216
Astatine	At	85	(210)
Barium	Ba	56	137.328
Berkelium	Bk	97	(247)
Beryllium	Be	4	9.0122
Bismuth	Bi	83	208.9804
Bohrium	Bh	107	(262)
Boron	B	5	10.81
Bromine	Br	35	79.904
Cadmium	Cd	48	112.412
Calcium	Ca	20	40.078
Californium	Cf	98	(251)
Carbon	C	6	12.011
Cerium	Ce	58	140.115
Cesium	Cs	55	132.9054
Chlorine	Cl	17	35.4528
Chromium	Cr	24	51.9962
Cobalt	Co	27	58.9332
Copper	Cu	29	63.546
Curium	Cm	96	(247)
Darmstadtium	Ds	110	(271)
Dubnium	Db	105	(262)
Dysprosium	Dy	66	162.5
Einsteinium	Es	99	(252)
Erbium	Er	68	167.26
Europium	Eu	63	151.966
Fermium	Fm	100	(257)
Fluorine	F	9	18.9984

ELEMENT	SYMBOL	ATOMIC NUMBER	ATOMIC MASS
Francium	Fr	87	(223)
Gadolinium	Gd	64	157.25
Gallium	Ga	31	69.723
Germanium	Ge	32	72.61
Gold	Au	79	196.9655
Hafnium	Hf	72	178.49
Hassium	Hs	108	(263)
Helium	He	2	4.0026
Holmium	Ho	67	164.9303
Hydrogen	H	1	1.00794
Indium	In	49	114.818
Iodine	I	53	126.9045
Iridium	Ir	77	192.217
Iron	Fe	26	55.845
Krypton	Kr	36	83.798
Lanthanum	La	57	138.9055
Lawrencium	Lr	103	(260)
Lead	Pb	82	207.2
Lithium	Li	3	6.941
Lutetium	Lu	71	174.967
Magnesium	Mg	12	24.3051
Manganese	Mn	25	54.938
Meitnerium	Mt	109	(268)
Mendelevium	Md	101	(258)
Mercury	Hg	80	200.59
Molybdenum	Mo	42	95.94
Neodymium	Nd	60	144.24
Neon	Ne	10	20.1798
Neptunium	Np	93	(237)
Nickel	Ni	28	58.6934
Niobium	Nb	41	92.9064
Nitrogen	N	7	14.0067
Nobelium	No	102	(259)

ELEMENT	SYMBOL	ATOMIC NUMBER	ATOMIC MASS
Osmium	Os	76	190.23
Oxygen	O	8	15.9994
Palladium	Pd	46	106.42
Phosphorus	P	15	30.9738
Platinum	Pt	78	195.08
Plutonium	Pu	94	(244)
Polonium	Po	84	(209)
Potassium	K	19	39.0938
Praseodymium	Pr	59	140.908
Promethium	Pm	61	(145)
Protactinium	Pa	91	231.036
Radium	Ra	88	(226)
Radon	Rn	86	(222)
Rhenium	Re	75	186.207
Rhodium	Rh	45	102.9055
Roentgenium	Rg	111	(272)
Rubidium	Rb	37	85.4678
Ruthenium	Ru	44	101.07
Rutherfordium	Rf	104	(261)
Samarium	Sm	62	150.36
Scandium	Sc	21	44.9559
Seaborgium	Sg	106	(266)
Selenium	Se	34	78.96

ELEMENT	SYMBOL	ATOMIC NUMBER	ATOMIC MASS
Silicon	Si	14	28.0855
Silver	Ag	47	107.8682
Sodium	Na	11	22.9898
Strontium	Sr	38	87.62
Sulfur	S	16	32.067
Tantalum	Ta	73	180.948
Technetium	Tc	43	(98)
Tellurium	Te	52	127.6
Terbium	Tb	65	158.9253
Thallium	Tl	81	204.3833
Thorium	Th	90	232.0381
Thulium	Tm	69	168.9342
Tin	Sn	50	118.711
Titanium	Ti	22	47.867
Tungsten	W	74	183.84
Ununbium	Uub	112	(277)
Uranium	U	92	238.0289
Vanadium	V	23	50.9415
Xenon	Xe	54	131.29
Ytterbium	Yb	70	173.04
Yttrium	Y	39	88.906
Zinc	Zn	30	65.409
Zirconium	Zr	40	91.224

GLOSSARY

Acid A compound that forms hydrogen ions (H^+) when dissolved in water.

Activation energy Energy needed to start a chemical reaction.

Activity series of metals A table listing metals in order of decreasing activity.

Anion Any atom or group of atoms with a negative charge.

Aqueous solution A solution in which chemicals are dissolved in water.

Atom The smallest particle of an element that still has all the chemical properties of the element; the basic building block of matter.

Atomic number The number of protons in the nucleus of an atom of an element.

Autotroph A producer—an organism that produces its own food using light or chemical energy instead of eating.

Base A compound that forms hydroxide ions (OH^-) when dissolved in water.

Bioluminescent The ability of a living organism to produce light.

Bohr model A model of the atom developed by Niels Bohr; resembles the solar system.

Carbohydrate Chemical compounds that contain carbon, hydrogen, and oxygen. Sugars and starches are carbohydrates.

Carbon-14 dating A technique used by scientists to determine the age of organic material.

Catalyst A substance that increases the rate of a chemical reaction without itself being changed in the chemical reaction.

Cation Any atom or group of atoms with a positive charge.

Chemical bond An attractive force that holds atoms in molecules or compounds.

Chemical change A rearrangement of atoms that results in the production of new substances; also called a chemical reaction.

Chemical formula A written expression using chemical symbols and numbers to show how atoms are joined.

Chemical equation A way to describe a chemical reaction using chemical formulas.

Chemical reaction A change that produces one or more new substances; also called a chemical change.

Chemical symbol A short way of writing the name of an element.

Chemiluminescence The generation of light as a result of a chemical reaction.

Chemosynthesis The process used by some bacteria and fungi to make their own food from chemicals, such as hydrogen sulfide.

Chlorophyll Green pigments in plants that convert sunlight into chemical energy. Chlorophyll is found in the chloroplasts of plant cells.

Chloroplast A special structure inside a plant cell where chlorophyll carries out photosynthesis.

Combination reaction A chemical reaction in which two reactants produce one product. It is also called a synthesis reaction.

Combustion Burning; oxygen is one of the reactants.

Complete combustion A combustion reaction that produces carbon dioxide and water as products.

Compound Two or more elements held together by chemical bonds.

Concentration The number of molecules in a given volume; the strength of a solution.

Covalent bond A bond between two or more atoms that involves sharing electrons. It often happens between two nonmetals.

Decomposition reaction A chemical reaction in which one reactant breaks down into two or more products. It has the general formula $Ax \rightarrow A + x$.

Diatomic element Elements that, in their natural state, always contain two atoms of the same element joined together by chemical bonds. The seven most common diatomic elements are fluorine, chlorine, bromine, iodine, hydrogen, nitrogen, and oxygen.

Digestion The process by which food is broken down into chemicals that can be absorbed by the body.

Double displacement reaction A chemical reaction in which two compounds swap ions. It has the general formula $Ax + By \rightarrow Ay + Bx$.

Double replacement reaction See double displacement reaction.

Ductile A physical property of metals, it is the capability of being drawn into wires without breaking.

Duodenum The top part of the small intestines that is attached to the stomach.

Electricity A form of energy produced by the flow of charged particles such as electrons or ions.

Electrochemical device Any device that converts chemical energy into electrical energy or electrical energy into chemical energy.

Electrolyte A substance that will conduct electricity when dissolved in water or melted. Acids, bases, and ionic compounds are common electrolytes.

Electron A negatively charged subatomic particle with almost no mass that can be found outside of the nucleus of an atom of an element.

Element A substance made of only one type of atom.

Endothermic reaction A chemical reaction that needs an input of energy to occur.

Energy level A region around the nucleus of an atom where an electron will most likely be moving.

Enzyme A biological catalyst; almost always a protein.

Exothermic reaction A chemical reaction that produces energy.

Fermentation The conversion of sugar to alcohol and carbon dioxide, performed by microbes.

Fission A nuclear reaction that results in the division of an atom's nucleus into at least two different nuclei. Large amounts of energy are released in this process.

Fusion A nuclear reaction that results in the fusing of two or more nuclei to form a more massive nuclei. Large amounts of energy are released in this process, which is also called a thermonuclear reaction.

Half-life The amount of time it takes for half of a radioactive substance to decay.

Halogen Any member of the nonmetallic elements in Group 17 of the periodic table. It includes the elements fluorine, chlorine, bromine, and iodine.

Hydrocarbon An organic compound that contains hydrogen and carbon.

Hydrothermal vent A place on the ocean floor where hot, chemical-filled water comes up from cracks in Earth's crust.

Incomplete combustion A combustion reaction in which not enough oxygen is present, resulting in unwanted byproducts such as soot, nitrous oxides, sulfur oxides, and carbon monoxide.

Inert Not chemically reactive under normal circumstances.

Inhibitor A substance that slows down a chemical reaction.

Insoluble Incapable of being dissolved.

Ion A positively or negatively charged atom or group of atoms.

Ionic bond A chemical bond in which electrons are transferred from one atom to another, forming electrically charged particles. Ionic bonds usually occur between a metal and a nonmetal.

Ionic salt A compound produced by the combining the cation from a base and the anion from an acid.

Isotope An atom that has the same number of protons in its nucleus as other atoms of the same element, but with a different number of neutrons, resulting in a different atomic mass.

Kinetic energy The energy an object has because of its motion.

Lactase An enzyme in the small intestines needed to digest lactose, a sugar found in milk.

Lactose A sugar found in milk.

Lactose intolerance A condition caused by the body's inability to make lactase and digest lactose.

Law of conservation of mass A scientific law that states that mass can neither be created nor destroyed during a chemical reaction.

Light-induced chemical reaction A type of chemical reaction that occurs when light is absorbed.

Lustrous Glossy, shiny.

Malleable A physical property of metals, the ability to be hammered into a sheet or bent, without breaking.

Mass The amount of matter in a substance, measured in grams or kilograms.

Mass number The sum of the number of protons and neutrons in the nucleus of an atom.

Matter Anything that takes up space and has mass.

Metal A class of elements that are characteristically lustrous, malleable, ductile, and good conductors of heat and electricity. Metals include the majority of known elements.

Microbe A microscopic organism, such as yeast or bacteria.

Mitochondria Specialized structures in cells that provide energy—the "power plant" of the cell.

Mole Measurement of the amount of a substance. One mole is equal to 6.02×10^{23} atoms, molecules, or formula units of a substance. One mole is also equal to the molecular weight of a substance in grams.

Molecule The smallest unit of a chemical compound that still has the same chemical properties of that compound.

Monomer The smallest part of a polymer. Chains of monomers make polymers.

Neutralization reaction A reaction in which an acid and a base react with one another to form water and an ionic salt, a neutral solution.

Neutron A subatomic particle with no charge and a mass of 1 atomic mass unit (amu), found in the nucleus of an atom.

Noble gas Any of the chemically inert gases in Group 18 of the periodic table. These gases have full outer energy levels.

Nonmetal A class of elements that are not lustrous and do not conduct heat or electricity well. They are grouped on the right side of the periodic table.

Nuclear reaction A reaction that changes the nucleus of an atom.

Nucleus The dense, positively charged center of an atom.

Octet rule A theory that states that atoms tend to form bonds in order to get eight electrons in their valence electron shell.

Organic Compounds containing carbon. The word *organic* also means of or relating to living things.

Oxidation reaction A reaction in which an element loses electrons. This kind of reaction cannot happen without a reduction reaction.

Oxidation-reduction reaction A reaction in which electrons are transferred between reactants; also called a redox reaction.

Oxidizing agent The substance in a redox reaction that accepts electrons. In a redox reaction, the oxidizing agent is reduced.

Patina A surface film caused by oxidation that appears on some metals over time. The film protects the underlying metal from further corrosion.

Photoautotroph An organism that produces its own food through photosynthesis, using energy from sunlight.

Photon A unit of electromagnetic energy seen as light.

Photosynthesis The process in which plants use the energy in sunlight to convert water and carbon dioxide into food for themselves, giving off oxygen as a result.

Physical change A change in what something looks like, but not what it is made of.

Polymer Large molecules formed by combining simpler molecules (monomers) in regular patterns.

Polymerization The process of forming a polymer.

Precipitate A solid compound that does not dissolve and is produced during a chemical reaction.

Product New substances formed as the result of a chemical reaction.

Propellant A fuel; a material used to produce a force in order to drive an object forward.

Proton A subatomic particle with a positive charge and a mass of 1 atomic mass unit (amu), found in the nucleus of an atom.

Quantum mechanical model The modern, more accurate model of the atom in which the chance of finding an electron in a certain position at any given time are calculated and plotted. The model resembles a fuzzy cloud.

Radioactive A property of some isotopes of certain elements that have unstable nuclei and are capable of giving off radiation, or breaking down.

Radioactive decay The natural process in which the unstable nuclei of some isotopes of certain elements give off energy in the form of radiation, eventually changing into a different, more stable, isotope.

Reactant Substances that react with one another in a chemical reaction to form new substances.

Reaction rate The speed with which a chemical reaction occurs.

Reducing agent The substance in a redox reaction that loses electrons. In a redox reaction, the reducing agent is oxidized.

Reduction reaction A reaction in which an element gains electrons. This cannot happen without an oxidation reaction.

Respiration A process in which an organism takes in oxygen and carbohydrates and gives off carbon dioxide, water, and energy that the organism needs to live.

Single displacement reaction A chemical reaction in which an element replaces one ion in a compound. It has the general formula $A + By \rightarrow Ay + B$.

Single replacement reaction See single displacement reaction.

Solute The substance that is dissolved by the solvent in a solution. For example, salt is the solute in salt water.

Solution A mixture made by dissolving a solid in a liquid.

Solvent A substance, usually a liquid, that can dissolve other substances. For example, water is the solvent in salt water.

Speleothem A cave formation.

Stalactite An icicle shaped cave formation that hangs from the ceiling.

Stalagmite A cone-shaped cave formation that is formed on the cave floor when water containing dissolved calcium carbonate drips from a cave's ceiling.

Static electricity An electrical charge produced by friction.

Subatomic particle A particle that is smaller than an atom. Subatomic particles include protons, neutrons, electrons, quarks, photons, neutrinos, and muons.

Symbiotic relationship A relationship between two organisms that benefits both.

Synthesis reaction A chemical reaction in which two reactants produce one product. It is also called a combination reaction.

Synthetic Human-made, artificial.

Thermogenesis The generation of heat.

Thermonuclear reaction Nuclear fusion.

Transmutation The conversion of one element into another as the result of a nuclear reaction.

Valence electrons Electrons in the outermost electron shell of an atom.

BIBLIOGRAPHY

"A Basic Overview of Fuel Cell Technology." Collecting the History of Fuel Cells: A Smithsonian Research Project. Smithsonian Institution. Available online. URL: http://americanhistory.si.edu/fuelcells/basics.htm. Accessed Dec. 17, 2006.

"About Bioluminescence." Lights Alive! San Diego Natural History Museum. Available online. URL: http://www.sdnhm.org/kids/lightsalive/biolum3.html. Accessed Dec. 17, 2006.

"Ammonium Perchlorate: Helping to Launch the Space Shuttle Discovery." The Science Center. The Chlorine Chemistry Council. Available online. URL: http://www.science-education.org/classroom_activities/chlorine_compound/ammonium_perch.html. Accessed Dec. 17, 2006.

Brain, Marshall. "How Carbon-14 Dating Works." Howstuffworks. Available online. URL: http://science.howstuffworks.com/carbon-14.htm. Accessed Dec. 17, 2006.

Branham, Marc. "Firefly Facts." The Firefly Files. Ohio State University. Available online. URL: http://iris.biosci.ohio-state.edu/projects/FFiles/frfact.html. Accessed Dec. 17, 2006.

Carpi, Anthony. "Chemical Bonding." Visionlearning. The National Science Foundation. Available online. URL: http://www.visionlearning.com/library/module_viewer.php?mid=55. Accessed Dec. 17, 2006.

Carpi, Anthony. "Nuclear Chemistry." Visionlearning. The National Science Foundation. Available online. URL: http://www.visionlearning.com/library/module_viewer.php?c3=&mid=59&l. Accessed Dec. 17, 2006.

Casiday, Rachel, and Regina Frey. "Chemistry Behind Airbags." Gas Laws Save Lives. Department of Chemistry, Washington University in St. Louis. Available online. URL: http://www.chemistry.wustl.edu/~edudev/LabTutorials/Airbags/airbags.html. Accessed Dec. 17, 2006.

Farabee, M. J. "Reactions & Enzymes." Online Biology Book. Estrella Mountain Community College. Available online. URL: http://www.emc.maricopa.edu/faculty/farabee/biobk/BioBookEnzym.html. Accessed Dec. 17, 2006.

"Food Safety Education." Foodsafetysite.com. North Carolina State University. Available online. URL: http://www.foodsafetysite.com/educators/competencies/general/microbiology/mic6.html. Accessed Dec. 17, 2006.

Freudenrich, Craig C. "How Fat Cells Work." Howstuffworks. Available online. URL: http://home.howstuffworks.com/fat-cell.htm. Accessed Dec. 17, 2006.

Gondhia, Reema. "The History of Fireworks." The Chemistry of Fireworks. The Royal Society of Chemistry. Available online. URL: http://www.chemsoc.org/ExemplarChem/entries/2004/icl_Gondhia/history.html. Accessed Dec. 17, 2006.

Haddock, S.H., C.M. McDougall, and J.F. Case. "The Bioluminescence Web Page." University of California at Santa Barbara. Available online. URL: http://www.lifesci.ucsb.edu/~biolum. Accessed Dec. 17, 2006.

Harris, Tom. "How Light Sticks Work." Howstuffworks. Available online. URL: http://science.howstuffworks.com/light-stick.htm. Accessed Dec. 17, 2006.

"How Airships Fly." American Blimp Corporation. Available online. URL: http://www.americanblimp.com/fly.htm. Accessed Dec. 17, 2006.

"How Does a Water Softener Work?" Howstuffworks. Available online. URL: http://home.howstuffworks.com/question99.htm. Accessed Dec. 17, 2006.

Hoyle, Brian. "Chemical Warfare." Encyclopedia of Espionage. Thomson Gale. Available online. URL: http://www.espionageinfo.com/Ch-Co/Chemical-Warfare.html. Accessed Dec. 17, 2006.

"Hydrothermal Vents." Voyage to the Deep. University of Delaware College of Marine Studies and Sea Grant College Program. Available online. URL: http://www.ocean.udel.edu/deepsea/level-2/geology/vents.html. Accessed Dec. 17, 2006.

"Kaboom!" Hot Science: It's Elemental! PBS/NOVA online. Available online. URL: http://www.pbs.org/wgbh/nova/kaboom/elemental. Accessed Dec. 17, 2006.

McGee, Elaine. "What is Acid Rain?" Acid Rain and Our Nation's Capital. U.S. Geological Survey. Available online. URL: http://pubs.usgs.gov/gip/acidrain/2.html. Accessed Dec. 17, 2006.

Nice, Karim. "How Fuel Cells Work." Howstuffworks. Available online. URL: http://www.howstuffworks.com/fuel-cell.htm. Accessed Dec. 17, 2006.

Ophardt, Charles. "Carbohydrates—Lactose." Virtual ChemBook. Chemistry Department, Elmhurst College. Available online. URL: http://www.elmhurst.edu/~chm/vchembook/546lactose.html. Accessed Dec. 17, 2006.

Palmer, Michael. "Brown Fat Tissue." Metabolism. University of Waterloo. Available online. URL: http://watcut.uwaterloo.ca/webnotes/Metabolism/page-10.2.6.html. Accessed Dec. 17, 2006.

Perlman, Howard. "Sinkholes." Water Science for Schools. U.S. Geological Survey. Available online. URL: http://ga.water.usgs.gov/edu/earthgwsinkholes.html. Accessed Dec. 17, 2006.

Pisarowicz, Jim. "Speleothems." Wind Cave National Park. National Park Service. Available online. URL: http://www.nps.gov/archive/wica/Speleothems.htm. Accessed Dec. 17, 2006.

"Polytetrafluoroethylene." Polymer Science Learning Center. Department of Polymer Science, The University of Southern Mississippi. Available online. URL: http://www.pslc.ws/mactest/ptfe.htm. Accessed Dec. 17, 2006.

"Roy J. Plunkett." Chemical Achievers: the Human Face of the Chemical Sciences. The Chemical Heritage Foundation.

Available online. URL: http://www.chemheritage.org/classroom/chemach/plastics/plunkett.html. Accessed Dec. 17, 2006.

"Science & Nature: Hot Topics—Cooking—Chemistry." BBC. Available online. URL: http://www.bbc.co.uk/science/hottopics/cooking/chemistry.shtml. Accessed Dec. 17, 2006.

Shakhashiri, Bassam. "Chemical of the Week—Fireworks!" Science is Fun in the Lab of Shakhashiri. University of Wisconsin-Madison. Available online. URL: http://scifun.chem.wisc.edu/chemweek/fireworks/fireworks.htm. Accessed Dec. 17, 2006.

"Statue Statistics." Statue of Liberty. National Park Service. Available online. URL: http://www.nps.gov/stli/historyculture/statue-statistics.htm. Accessed Dec. 17, 2006.

"The Hindenburg Disaster: Titanic of the Sky." Vidicom Media Productions. Available online. URL: http://www.vidicom-tv.com/tohiburg.htm. Accessed Dec. 17, 2006.

Tyson, Peter. "Fading Away." Saving the National Treasures. NOVA online. Available online. URL: http://www.pbs.org/wgbh/nova/charters/fading.html. Accessed Dec. 17, 2006.

Tyson, Peter. "Living At Extremes." Into the Abyss. NOVA online. Available online. URL: http://www.pbs.org/wgbh/nova/abyss/life/extremes.html. Accessed Dec. 17, 2006.

"What Is Electricity?" EIA Energy Kid's Page. Energy Information Administration. Available online. URL: http://www.eia.doe.gov/kids/energyfacts/sources/electricity.html. Accessed Dec. 17, 2006.

"What Makes a Firefly Glow?" Learn.Genetics. The University of Utah. Available online. URL: http://learn.genetics.utah.edu/units/basics/firefly. Accessed Dec. 17, 2006.

"Why Do Bruised or Cut Fruits (Bananas, Apples) Get Brown?" Food-Info.Net. Wageningen University, The Netherlands. Available online. URL: http://www.food-info.net/uk/qa/qa-fp138.htm. Accessed Dec. 17, 2006.

Winkler, Peter, ed. "Polymers—They're Everywhere." National Geographic Society. Available online. URL: http://www.nationalgeographic.com/education/plastics/index.html. Accessed Dec. 17, 2006.

"World War One—Weapons." History on the Net. Available online. URL: http://www.historyonthenet.com/WW1/weapons.htm. Accessed Dec. 17, 2006.

FURTHER READING

Baldwin, Carol. *Chemical Reactions*. Chicago: Raintree, 2004.

Breidahl, Harry. *Extremophiles: Life in Extreme Environments*. New York: Chelsea House Publishers, 2001.

Firestone, Mary. *Pyrotechnician*. New York: Chelsea House Publishers, 2005.

Hopkins, William G. *Photosynthesis and Respiration*. New York: Chelsea House Publishers, 2006.

Kidd, Jerry S., and Renee A. Kidd. *Nuclear Power: The Study of Quarks and Sparks*. New York: Chelsea House Publishers, 2006.

Lindop, Laurie. *Cave Sleuths: Solving Science Underground*. Minneapolis, Minn.: 21st Century Books, 2004.

Miller, Ron. *The Elements*. Minneapolis, Minn.: 21st Century Books, 2004.

Newmark, Ann. *Chemistry*. New York: DK Publishing, Inc., 2005.

Oxlade, Chris. *Acids and Bases*. Chicago: Heinemann Library, 2002.

Oxlade, Chris. *Materials Changes & Reactions*. Chicago: Heinemann Library, 2002.

Parker, Steve. *Break It Down: The Digestive System*. Chicago: Raintree, 2006.

Saunders, Nigel, and Steven Chapman. *Energy Essentials: Energy Transfers*. Chicago: Raintree, 2005.

Stille, Darlene R. *Chemical Change: From Fireworks to Rust*. Minneapolis, Minn.: Compass Point Books, 2005.

Walker, Niki. *Hydrogen: Running on Water*. New York: Crabtree Publishing Company, 2006.

Worth, Richard. *Gunpowder*. New York: Chelsea House Publishers, 2003.

Web Sites

The American Chemical Society

http://www.chemistry.org/kids

The American Chemical Society's Web site contains hands-on activities, interactive games, and articles.

The Atom's Family

http://www.miamisci.org/af/sln

This resource contains educational activities relating to different forms of energy. Each monster member of the Atom's Family introduces a topic, such as electricity and electrical safety (Frankenstein), the properties of light (Dracula), and fuel conservation and energy transfer (the Wolf Man).

NOVA Online

http://www.pbs.org/wgbh/nova

NOVA's companion Web site includes background information, supplemental information, and interactive resources for NOVA programs.

The pH Factor

http://www.miamisci.org/ph

This lesson on acids and bases includes hands-on activities such as cleaning pennies, using pH indicators, making invisible ink, and mapping the tongue's taste buds.

Rader's Chem4Kids.com

http://www.chem4kids.com/index.html

This site has basic information about matter, atoms, elements, everyday reactions, and biochemistry.

Science News for Kids

http://www.sciencenewsforkids.org

Read up-to-date science news articles and do hands-on activities, puzzles, and games. Topics on the site include animals, chemistry, dinosaurs, the environment, health, space, and weather.

Understanding Our Planet through Chemistry

http://minerals.cr.usgs.gov/gips/aii-home.htm

This U.S. Geological Survey site explores ways chemists use analytical chemistry to determine Earth's age, understand how pollution and acid rain affect Earth's plants and animals, and how the planet's climate has changed over thousands of years.

PHOTO CREDITS

Page:

2a: © Shutterstock [Jason Figert]
2b: © Shutterstock [Nikolay Okhitin]
2c: © Shutterstock [Jerry Callaghan]
4: © Shutterstock [Bob Ainsworth]
6: © Shutterstock [Anita Patterson Peppers]
10: © Shutterstock [Andril Oleksiienko]
14: © Lawrence Migdale / Photo Researchers, Inc.
24a: © Andrew Lambert Photography / Photo Researchers, Inc.
24b: © Charles D. Winters / Photo Researchers, Inc.
24c: © Shutterstock [Kimberly Hall]
28: © Infobase Publishing
29: © Infobase Publishing
31: © Infobase Publishing
33: © Infobase Publishing
39: © Infobase Publishing
42: © Infobase Publishing
49: © L.S. Stepanowicz / Visuals Unlimited
53: © Infobase Publishing
59: © Cliff Schiappa / AP Photo
60: © Infobase Publishing
61: © Infobase Publishing
67: © Shutterstock [Joshua Haviv]
70: © Dr. Bob Embley / NOAA PMEL / NOAA Office of Ocean Exploration
73: © E. Widder / HBOI / Visuals Unlimited
76a: © Shutterstock [Thomas Nord]
76b: © Shutterstock [Xavier Marchant]
80: © Shutterstock [David Watkins]

Cover:

© Charles D. Winters / Photo Researchers, Inc.

INDEX

ABOUT THE AUTHOR

KRISTI LEW is a former high-school science teacher with degrees in biochemistry and genetics. After years in the classroom and genetics laboratories, she is now the owner of a professional K–12 educational writing service that specializes in writing textbook chapters, magazine articles, and non-fiction books for students and teachers in all fields of science.